FAITHFUL

A BIBLICAL REFLECTION ON THEIR DAILY LIFE-STRUGGLES

ARE THE YOUTH

Written by

ADLChild of ElohimADL

Faithful Are The Youth

ISBN: 978-1-970055-03-0

Printed and bound
by
CreaTech Services, LLC
San Antonio, Texas
www.createchservices.net

Don't be dejected and sad, for the joy of the LORD is your strength! **(Nehemiah 8:10 NLT)**

I am the way, the truth, and the life. No one can come to the Father except through me. **(John 14:6 NLT)**

Need someone to listen; speak to God.

Turbulent times; hold on to God.

Hard times; have faith in God.

Happy times; rejoice in God.

Uncertain times; seek God.

Easy times; thank God.

All times; praise God.

Legal Disclaimer

This book is designed to provide a reflection of the daily life-struggles, biblical uplifting, and encouraging scriptures to our youth. The biblical information therein is taken from the **New Living Translation (NLT)**. The information provided in this book is designed to provide helpful information on the daily life-struggles discussed. The reading and reference materials in this book are informational and are meant for the general purpose of the reader. The information contained therein is not meant for medical treatment or diagnoses of medical symptoms. If you are experiencing medical problems, or if you have additional questions before or after reading this book, please contact your health care provider or physician. Help Resources provided are for informational purposes only and do not constitute an endorsement of any website or organization. Websites and telephone numbers listed in this book are subject to change. The author and/or publisher of this book are not responsible or liable to any person reading or following the information in this book.

Chapters:
1. Self-Esteem and Body Image
2. Emotional Health
3. Self-Identity
4. Depression and Suicide

Chapters:
9. Bullying
10. Peer and Parental Pressure
11. Competition
12. Poverty

Chapters:
5. Eating Disorders
6. Teen Pregnancy
7. Single-Parent Households
8. Child Abuse

Chapters:
13. Cyber Addiction
14. Alcohol and Drug Abuse
15. Premarital Sex

CONTENTS

For God has not given us a spirit of fear and timidity, but of power, love, and self-discipline. ***(2 Timothy 1:7 NLT)***

Introduction

He alone is my rock and my salvation, my fortress where I will not be shaken. ***(Psalm 62:6 NLT)***

Thank you for taking the time to read this book. The book was written and intended to shed light on the daily life-struggles faced by our youth. I applied biblical scriptures to demonstrate how the word of God applies to our struggles. My hope is this book uplifts you (our youth) and … fingers crossed, lead you to "spiritual growth." What is spiritual growth? I intend to elaborate on spiritual growth in a moment. But first, I share with you the "daily life-struggles." We have all gone through one or more of these struggles at some point or stage in our lives: Self-Esteem and Body Image, Emotional Health, Self-Identity, Depression and Suicide, Eating Disorders, Teen Pregnancy, Single-Parent Households, Child Abuse, Bullying, Peer and Parental Pressure, Competition, Poverty, Cyber Addiction, Alcohol and Drug Abuse, and Premarital Sex.

Although these struggles are different, one struggle can influence or lead to another. As a case in point, premarital sex may lead to teen pregnancy and result in a single-parent household for the child. Daily life-struggles do not discriminate. Regardless if you are of African, Asian, Indian, Arab, or European descent; Transgender, Male, or Female; Bisexual, Heterosexual, or Homosexual; none of it matters because many of the daily life-struggles affect your way of life and well-being. I was exposed to the harsh realities of the world. As a teenager, I placed witnessed and lived a few of the daily life-struggles: Poverty, Alcohol and Drug Abuse, Emotional Health, Competition, Single-Parent Households, and Premarital Sex. Although it occurred many years ago, I am still inspired by the daily life-struggles and perseverance of my family who rose above and triumphed. This experience stayed with me always. The experience stimulated my love of helping people and provided the motivation to write this book.

I first became interested in writing this book while volunteering as a youth mentor. Assuming the responsibility of mentoring a male teen growing up in a single-parent household without a father was all the motivation I needed to say, YES! I said yes and provided a young man an opportunity many are not privileged to have. A positive role model and father figure in their lives to show them how to become a responsible and respectable man. Being a man is difficult. One of the hardest decisions is standing firm by your principles and values when society disapproves. The fundamentals of becoming a man include politeness and respect, live by values and principles, be independent, possess integrity, not being afraid to accept the responsibilities of a man, listen to others with wisdom, and most of all, accept Jesus Christ as LORD and Savior. Allow me this opportunity to share with you my first candid experience as a youth mentor. For identity and privacy reasons, I will refer to this young man as Emmanuel.

Story: *The desire for helping people facing adversity runs through my veins. There were moments when I thought of solving world hunger or easing the series of pain people experienced. This was an enormous feat for an ordinary being. A big heart thumped inside of me and although the future was filled with uncertainties, I embodied this desire. I was too young to understand what this feeling meant. I only knew God placed it deep within me. Perhaps this desire was embedded during my days of living in and through poverty. When the opportunity presented itself to become a youth mentor, I could not resist.*

Selecting the best-suited youth mentoring program took several months. It pleased me to learn countless organizations were offering this service to support our youth. I researched many mentoring programs before I decided. I based the decision to commit on my available free-time, positive reputation of the organization, giving back to society, an opportunity to improve a mentee's self-esteem, and achieve personal growth.

The day of the interview took place in early winter. I remembered the brisk wintry morning and a feeling of excitement followed me as I arrived at the interview office. The receptionist courteously greeted and escorted me to the waiting area in the lobby. The office walls were filled with photographs of mentors and mentees displaying relationships of happiness.

The interviewer came out to welcome me and within a few short minutes, they escorted me to a room. The interviewer was a young male and looked approximately 15 years my junior. A series of personal questions were asked at the beginning of the interview. During the exchange of questions and answers, the interviewer revealed he was a former member of the youth mentoring program. He was once a mentee in search of a mentor. The interviewer displayed his gratitude for the program and volunteering was his way of giving back to a program that rescued him from the uncertainties of growing up without a father.

As the interview progressed, the questions became emotionally perplexed. The interviewer asked a specific question. "How do you feel about mentoring a high school junior who suffers from Bipolar disorder and is also part of the Juvenile Justice System?" Emmanuel did not have his biological father actively in his life and was known for smoking marijuana in school, skipping classes, and being arrested for possession of marijuana on the school campus. I took a few deep breaths and gathered my thoughts. I needed to be sure my next few words were of sound judgment and not emotional. "What do you mean by the Juvenile Justice System?" I asked. The interviewer looked at me with dismay as he contemplated a response. He cleared his throat and said, "Emmanuel is part of the Juvenile Justice System." His facial expressions portrayed a feeling of panic and the fear of losing an opportunity to find a mentor for Emmanuel.

Emmanuel's misfortune of not having a role model or father figure in his life led me to a decision. "I do not mind if Emmanuel is part of the Juvenile Justice System," in a kind response. I was more concerned about society's stance on teenagers being incarcerated. Do they deserve a second chance? What would Jesus Christ do in this situation? A revelation came to me. I realized mentees participating in this program needed guidance and emotional support. If mentees had a mother and father both actively taking part in their lives, they would not be in this mentorship program. This realization led me to respond confidently. "When do I begin?" "In a few weeks," the interviewer replied.

As the weeks came to pass, I received a telephone voice message informing me of a date and time. The message informed me to meet Emmanuel at his home for an initial meet-and-greet introduction. I remembered driving to Emmanuel's home on a Saturday morning. The part of town he lived in was unpleasant to the eyes. It was not safe and unwise to be there pass late-night hours due to high crime. I drove up to the front of his home and immediately saw what reminded me of growing up in poverty. The home displayed visible signs of damage and its appearance confirmed the neighborhood had seen better days. Although the neighborhood was unpleasant to the human eyes, I understood his living conditions and could relate to the struggles of poverty.

A feeling of nervousness flowed through me as I approached his doorsteps. I could not help but wonder if I made the right decision. Emmanuel's mother opened the door and greeted me with a smile and hug ... and more hugs! She unveiled a sense of relief because Emmanuel was waiting for a mentor for almost two years. I observed the inside of his home and they filled it with warmth as I sat and waited. Although his family lacked the financial means to acquire nice furniture, the family photos hanging on the imperfect walls supported a structured home of love and peace.

Emmanuel's mother made her way to his bedroom and alerted him of my arrival. He was just getting out of bed. The time was approaching noon, and it came of no surprise in learning of a teenager sleeping in on the weekend. With eyes fixated down the hallway, I gazed in suspense. I saw what appeared to be a grown man walking towards me. Emmanuel was over 6 feet tall and weighed no less than 220 pounds. As he towered over me and wiped his eyes, he said, "Hello big brother." I stood up in his towering presence and we embraced with a hug. He was just a child. I realized his reputation of being in the Juvenile Justice System was not a fair and reasonable assessment of his character. The young man I met was filled with love and happiness. He deserved a second chance.

Since our initial introduction, Emmanuel has made a full 360-turnaround in his life. He is no longer in the Juvenile Justice System, drug-free, and poised to graduate high school. Emmanuel has dreams and aspirations of enlisting in the United States Air Force. I am grateful the LORD allowed me an opportunity to mentor Emmanuel before it was too late. While I had the opportunity to mentor Emmanuel, I wrote this book as a platform to reach the millions of youths I cannot mentor in person. ***End***.

The experience gained as a youth mentor taught me that when we are submerged in positive influences of a caring adult; the outcome is extremely beneficial. Over the years, I learned how to establish a healthy work-life balance between career and family. This has evolved into regularly volunteering to help people experiencing daily life-struggles. It is amazing how much you can help others by listening to them speak about their struggles. People want to be heard and although listening may not solve their struggles, it offers them an outlet to express their feelings. Why am I sharing this information with you? I wanted to let you know that you are not alone, and people do care and love you. Have faith and trust in the LORD because he sees and knows all things.

Let us revisit Spiritual Growth. This requires us to become more like Christ, and there is no other way around it. How can I accomplish Spiritual Growth? Am I strong enough? How much discipline does it require? To answer these questions and others you are thinking of at this very moment, I recommend incorporating the following four suggestions into your daily living:

1) Minimalize your regularity and harshness of sin…

2) Increase your awareness and understanding of our Heavenly Father, God…

3) Always keep the faith and trust in God…

4) Apply Christ-like qualities in your daily life…

This is easier said than done, right?

If your answer is yes, I agree with you one hundred percent. It is difficult to flip a switch and turn your life around without dedicated commitment, effort, and prayer.

The truth is…

This is a lifelong commitment and requires a dedicated effort. An achievable first step is to visit your local church or ministry and ask, "How do I become more like Christ?"

This book covers significant daily life-struggles broken down into 4 sections and includes 15 chapters. Each of the daily life-struggles is explained thoroughly and supported by biblical scriptures to highlight its relevance and applicability. Chapter 1 focuses on ***Self-Esteem and Body Image.*** Chapter 2 focuses on ***Emotional Health.*** Chapter 3 focuses on ***Self-Identity.*** Chapter 4 focuses on ***Depression and Suicide.*** Chapter 5 focuses on ***Eating Disorders.*** Chapter 6 focuses on ***Teen Pregnancy.*** Chapter 7 focuses on ***Single-Parent Households.*** Chapter 8 focuses on ***Child Abuse.*** Chapter 9 focuses on ***Bullying.*** Chapter 10 focuses on ***Peer and Parental Pressure.*** Chapter 11 focuses on ***Competition.*** Chapter 12 focuses on ***Poverty.*** Chapter 13 focuses on ***Cyber Addiction.*** Chapter 14 focuses on ***Alcohol and Drug Abuse.*** *And,* Chapter 15 focuses on ***Premarital Sex.***

Each of the 15 chapters includes literature on the daily life-struggles, a biblical scripture breakdown of each struggle, a prayer section, related biblical scriptures, help resources, and 6 steps to building a relationship with God. Suggestions on how to use this book are listed on the next page.

How to Use this Book

1. This book is organized into **15** chapters and explains each of the daily life-struggles (*Self-Esteem and Body Image, Emotional Health, Self-Identity, Depression and Suicide, Eating Disorders, Teen Pregnancy, Single-Parent Households, Child Abuse, Bullying, Peer and Parental Pressure, Competition, Poverty, Cyber Addiction, Alcohol and Drug Abuse, and Premarital Sex*). I encourage you to read all chapters or choose the chapter(s) most applicable to your situation.

2. Whether you read all chapters or the most applicable, you will find each chapter covering:

a) An explanation of the struggle.

b) An interpretation of applicable biblical scriptures for the struggle and how it applies.

c) A written prayer section is available for you to follow, unique to the struggle. If you choose to, you may follow your prayer from the heart.

d) Related scriptures are available at the end of each chapter to attain additional biblical knowledge.

e) At your discretion, a listing of professional help resources is available at the end of each chapter for you to contact with questions about your daily life-struggle.

3. Each chapter has **6** recommended steps for building a relationship with God.

4. If you have biblical questions, concerns, or desire to learn more once you have read any or all chapters, I recommend:

a) Contact your local church ministry and/or pick up a copy of the Holy Bible. Begin reading to learn more about the scriptures or general inquiries about the bible. If you are not a member of a local church, pray to Jesus Christ for guidance and follow your heart in finding the church and religion of your calling. The key is to inquire about the LORD, and he will lead you down the correct path to salvation.

b) If you are not ready to contact your local church ministry, start by praying at home and reading the Holy Bible. When you are ready for the next step, the LORD will welcome you with open arms.

c) If neither of the daily life-struggles in this book applies to your situation, and you need to speak to someone, contact your local church ministry or professional health care services. If you are experiencing an emergency, contact your local authorities (crisis centers, police departments, medical treatment centers, councilors, etc.) for immediate help.

Now that you have read a preview of what is to come in this book, let us move on to the first section and begin reading Chapter 1 to learn of the challenges faced regarding ***Self-Esteem and Body Image*** and what the Holy Scripture revealed!

SECTION I

CHAMPIONING YOUR INNER SELF

My old self has been crucified with Christ. It is no longer I who live, but Christ lives in me. **(Galatians 2:20 NLT)**

Chapter 1

Self-Esteem and Body Image

The LORD doesn't see things the way you see them. People judge by outward appearance, but the LORD looks at the heart. **(1 Samuel 16:7 NLT)**

There are many questions about self-esteem and body image, and the frequent body changes you experience as a youth. Am I too short? Do I look attractive? Am I accepted by peers? Take a moment to consider and write down a listing of questions you might have.

____

____

____

____

____

When you reflect on the many questions about self-esteem and body image, the time spent pondering and wishing affects your self-image. This is due in part because as your body changes, it affects your being entirely. The snowball effect is, as you evaluate yourself in a certain way, you sometimes feel your peers view you the same. As a youth going through changes, including hormonal, you view the world differently especially if you are having trouble adjusting. Oftentimes mood swings accompany these changes and negatively impact your friends and family. Mood swings may also stem from a lack of sleep, anxiety, fatigue, and poor dieting. The feeling of superiority tends to come with being a youth, however, it is important to take care of your mind and body through a healthy diet and plenty of rest.

Adults experienced the same adverse feelings stemming from self-esteem and body image during their days as a youth. Today, adults still experience these symptoms. The main difference is adults are more experienced and equipped to deal with the side effects. Although adults are better equipped, it does not mean they emotionally hurt less or immune to the negative effects. Have you ever turned on the television or traversed the internet only to discover you find yourself comparing your physical features to those of the people you see? Does this progress into comparing yourself to peers? What if you are smaller in size or shorter in comparison to what you see? The danger of doing this is, if you do not meet the standards you see, it affects your well-being and self-esteem. The result tends to be the development of low self-esteem.

"Confront the dark parts of yourself, and work to banish them with illumination and forgiveness. Your willingness to wrestle with your demons will cause your angels to sing."

— August Wilson

Source: https://motivateus.com/cibt-27.htm

Some of the symptoms associated with low self-esteem include feelings of shyness, negative attitude, depression, insecurity, withdrawal, and irritation. For example, shyness affects how you feel or conduct yourself around other people. This means you feel uncomfortable and nervous. Having low self-esteem or unhappiness with your body image does not mean it is the end of the world. If you surround yourself with positive people who uplift you with encouraging words, this instantly changes your mood to view the world in an entirely different way. However, it is not easy. It requires effort on your part.

As a positive first step forward, communicate with people you trust. Use this opportunity as a platform to express your thoughts or feelings. Have you ever thought about going to your local church and joining a ministry to talk about how you are feeling? Take a leap of faith and give Jesus Christ a chance to intervene. *If you are faithful in little things, you will be faithful in large ones* ***(Luke 16:10 NLT)***. I remember experiencing self-esteem and body image struggles as a youth. It was a difficult time for me because I thought no one understood what I was going through. I was often embarrassed or shy around strangers and visitors who came to my home. I felt this way because it meant interacting with people outside of my circle and comfort zone. I was very comfortable around friends and family. However, when it came to strangers or visitors, I thought they would see all my perceived flaws. Some of the perceived flaws included ungroomed hair, body shape, large teeth, large stomach, etc. Those perceived flaws led to low self-esteem.

Overcoming these struggles begins with God. This involves establishing a relationship with God through prayer. *There has never been a day like this one before or since, when the LORD answered such a prayer* ***(Joshua 10:14 NLT)***. Attending church as a youth was not my preferred thing and the day I began praying was awkward. I did not know how to pray, and it began with the fumbling of words. As the time came to pass, my relationship with God became stronger by the minute. The feeling of shyness disappeared and my love for him grew. As my self-esteem increased, my belief in him strengthened.

The second action taken was to ignore negative comments people made about me. How do you accomplish this? The best way is to reduce or avoid personal contact with negative people. There is no point hanging around people who intentionally drain your positive energy and intend to cause you turmoil. As my grandmother always said to me, “Misery loves company.” The combination of building a relationship with God and blocking out negative comments truly made a difference for me. The LORD will not get hung up on your self-esteem and body image. He welcomes you and accepts you for who you are. Why? He loves all his children, including you. The LORD understands what you are going through, and I can attest with certainty he will help you.

Let us reflect on what the Holy Scripture reveals: *The LORD doesn't see things the way you see them. People judge by outward appearance, but the LORD looks at the heart* ***(1 Samuel 16:7 NLT)***. The scripture states the LORD doesn't *see* things the way you see them. What does this mean? Let us begin and focus on the word "see." As human beings, we all see things entirely differently from others. This can be said for the way we perceive the weather for example. At 75 degrees Fahrenheit, some people may feel this temperature as cool, while others may feel this to be warm. What remains unchanged is the temperature. It is still 75 degrees Fahrenheit.

As you see self-esteem and body image as a daily life-struggle, the LORD sees this as an opportunity for spiritual growth in you. God is trying to open your eyes and let you see things his way, in a positive light. He wants you to take a different approach to confront this struggle. He wants you to turn to him and ask for intervention in the way you perceive yourself. In turn, Jesus Christ will place you on a path of self-discovery and acceptance. And second, the LORD said, "*People judge by outward appearance.*" We are all guilty of judging each other based on what we see externally. If we see a celebrity in the limelight, our perception is oftentimes positive. We may perceive this celebrity as looking flawless, wealthy, famous, and living a perfect life.

On the contrary, some celebrities experience self-esteem and body image struggles because internally they are unhappy with how they are perceived. The LORD is saying he will not judge your outward appearance because this does not matter to him. He is only focusing on your heart. As the scripture reads, "*But the LORD looks at the heart.*" The LORD sees you for the beautiful person you are, and he wants to use you as a radiant glow of his Holy Spirit shining bright for the rest of the world to see.

YOU ARE ON THE PREDETERMINED PATH set forth by the LORD. Most people believe daily outcomes are based on a chain of events dependent on one another. They forget the LORD is the sole reason and purpose behind every daily outcome. There is no better time or place like the present to submerge one's self in God's cloak of faith. He has no limitations or boundaries in his arsenal of gifts. There is no coincidence or chance about your life. Switch your focus to the LORD and allow every moment of your days to draw closer to him. As you listen to his direction of peace, you are equipped to travel the path set forth for you. Transitioning your inner thoughts from self-esteem and body image over to constant communication with the LORD, you will discover a better way to make it through the day.

Prepare Your Heart for the LORD's Prayer!

Let us pray: LORD, thank you for the daily life-struggle of self-esteem and body image. Thank you for giving me this opportunity to witness your greatness. To witness that no matter the struggle, you are beside me, behind me, and in front of me leading the way. I know LORD that you created me in your perfect image, and I should love myself for who I am. Some days LORD I struggle to accept myself, but today is a new day. The struggles of yesterday are now a distant memory.

Today is filled with new hope for our lifelong journey together. I am honored to know I have a God who has no boundaries or limitations in this world we live in. I submit my struggle to you. I submit my life to you, knowing my struggle is in your Holy Hands. Today and this day forth, I will do my best to follow your lead. When I stumble or have doubts, please forgive me, LORD. Help me develop a faith in you that is immovable by any struggle I face. I pray for my life this day forth is filled with your grace, love, and peace. In Jesus' name, in Jesus' name, AMEN!

Building a Relationship with God
1. Begin praying at home 2. Find a place of worship (church) 3. Attend church weekly 4. Join a church ministry and participate monthly 5. Ask Jesus Christ his purpose for you 6. Accept Jesus Christ as your LORD and Savior

Now that you have read about ***Self-Esteem and Body Image***, continue reading onto Chapter 2 to learn of the challenges faced regarding ***Emotional Health*** and what the Holy Scripture revealed.

Related Scriptures
So God created human beings in his own image. In the image of God he created them; male and female he created them. **(Genesis 1:27 NLT)** All of you together are Christ's body, and each of you is a part of it. **(1 Corinthians 12:27 NLT)** To whom can you compare God? What image can you find to resemble him? **(Isaiah 40:18 NLT)** Christ is the visible image of the invisible God. He existed before anything was created and is supreme over all creation. **(Colossians 1:15 NLT)**

Self-Esteem and Body Image Help Resources
Eating Disorders Awareness and Prevention (1-800-931-2237) Eating Disorders Center (1-888-236-1188) National Association of Anorexia Nervosa and Associated Disorders (1-847-831-3438)

Chapter 2

Emotional Health

Even if we feel guilty, God is greater than our feelings, and he knows everything. ***(1 John 3:20 NLT)***

Have you ever felt like you are on top of the world? Do you feel at peace and no obstacle placed on your path can derail you? How about the natural ability to tackle life obstacles without fail … do you possess it? If you answered any of these questions with a profound "Yes!" you are probably an emotionally healthy person. Why? When you are an emotionally healthy person, you are equipped to control your emotions and manner. For other people, it is a constant struggle dealing with obstacles the world has to offer. Some of these obstacles may include lack of inspiration, fear of failure, fear of disappointment, lack of emotional support, lack of desire, or lack of passion.

To illustrate, you might experience a lack of inspiration in your personal life, resulting in missed opportunities. This may come to fruition in the form of failing to apply for a job before the submission deadline and consequently missing out on a great job opportunity. If you are unable to deal with these obstacles and other challenges, to include establishing and nurturing relationships, adapting to world-changing events, organically possessing self-confidence, or having a sense of purpose, you might not be of good emotional health.

"Emotional healing requires more than simply changing how you feel. Your emotions are merely symptoms of the problem - not the problem itself. Even when they hurt."

— Jessica Moore

Source: https://www.goodreads.com/quotes/tag/emotional-health

---

Hormonal changes affect your body and could add to the complexities of confronting and managing daily obstacles of the world. These hormonal changes adversely impact your emotional health, and as a result, may lead to mood swings and perhaps a complete emotional breakdown (nervous breakdown). Although symptoms are temporary, experiencing a nervous breakdown is extremely difficult to cope with and seeking medical attention is a top priority.

Stressful situations including academic pressure, parental pressure, and peer pressure are situations that could lead to a breakdown. Have you felt incapable of fulfilling parental or peer expectations? If so, approaching this with a positive attitude is a good start and understanding that achieving emotional health will not happen overnight but through prayer, dedication, and positive thinking and emotions. *Always be full of joy in the Lord. I say it again, rejoice* ***(Philippians 4:4 NLT)***. Do not be afraid to face negative emotions and remember hiding them is counterproductive to establishing emotional health.

During my life's journey, I faced many personal fears deemed insurmountable. For instance, I lived with the fear of not excelling in school and meeting family expectations. I understood at an early age that an education is needed to gain knowledge and learn basic skills to function in the real world. The stress of achieving good grades in school always weighted on me and felt overwhelming.

There were moments where I felt life was not fair or things happened to me without justifiable cause. The truth is … I was not emotionally equipped to handle what life tossed at me. I wanted to toss my life obstacles back. But who could I have tossed it to? I did not want friends or family to know how ill-equipped I was in dealing with life obstacles. I did what seemed the most rational. I kept asking, "Why Me LORD!" At that moment, I did not realize how these three words, "Why" "Me" "LORD" would become the beginning of a lifelong relationship with Jesus Christ, and a fresh outlook on life obstacles.

Those three words evolved into prayers and a comforting foundation to rest my weary feet. As a youth, my grandparents often told me to attend church, but I did not want to listen. I thought I was matured and physically strong enough to conquer life obstacles on my own. However, I was not emotionally equipped to achieve it or brave enough to admit I could not do it on my own. I applied some approaches taught and learned from my grandparents and other family members:

1. **Think positive**. Remind yourself how emotionally strong you are, and you will develop enough courage to conquer any obstacle on your path.
2. **Surround yourself with positive people**. Remember, if someone has never won a battle, they are not equipped to tell you how to win the war.
3. **Seek Jesus Christ**. There is no right way, appropriate setting, or convenient time to reach out to him. Just do it!

What are other approaches do you believe can be adopted in your life? Take a moment to consider and write them down.

____

____

____

____

____

I pray you find courage and talk to your family, friends, or just reach out in prayers to Jesus Christ and ask him to show you the way.

Let us reflect on what the Holy Scripture reveals: *Even if we feel guilty, God is greater than our feelings, and he knows everything* ***(1 John 3:20 NLT)***. The scripture starts out sharing with us the feeling of *guilt*. But why do we feel this way?

We may feel guilty for many reasons. Perhaps we did something against our moral code. As a case in point, you might have violated that moral code when you lied to your parents about cleaning your room or staying away from risqué internet websites.

The scripture reveals, *"God is greater than our feelings."* He looks beyond your feelings because he has a greater purpose for you. This does not imply he neglects how you feel. No, he cares deeply for his children and our emotional health. The LORD wants you to be in good emotional health, so you can focus on him and the purpose he lays forth for you. The LORD went on to say, *"He knows everything."* This means he understands your emotional health is a constant struggle and needs you to let him into your life. He wants to comfort you through his teachings of spiritual guidance and growth.

The LORD knows you need strength to triumph, and he is ready to empower you. There is no better time than today to ask our LORD and Savior Jesus Christ for help with your daily life-struggle. Ask him to lift the load off your conscience and carry it for you. Why? The LORD is more than capable of taking care of his children, you.

GO TO THE LORD with an open heart and prepare yourself to receive his abundant grace, blessings, and everlasting love. He knows the complexity and extensiveness of your emotional health. The journey so far has been difficult, depriving you of the simple joys in life. The moment is here for you to go to him for comfort. Let the LORD remove the weight from your weary feet and place you in a state of relief. Moments of need allow the LORD to display his limitless power of gifts to those who seek it. When you lose sight of the LORD's presence, whisper his name and make him once again the focal point.

Prepare Your Heart for the LORD's Prayer!

Let us pray: LORD, as I come to you today with heavy thoughts on my mind regarding my emotional health, I want to ask for your help. I ask that you give me the mental strength to make it through this day. The burden is too heavy for my emotions to withstand. I need you my LORD and Savior Jesus Christ. Show me the way along this foggy road of uncertainty. I want to see beyond the haze and focus on your beacon light of hope. Yes LORD, show me what victory looks like on the horizon so my heart may burst with gratitude. As I give my trust to you, I know you will not lead me astray. I know you will comfort me every step along this journey to emotional health.

When I travel off course LORD, nudge me back onto the straight and narrow path. I do not want to lose time. The journey is long, but time is even more precious. I do not want to miss a moment of what you have in store for me. I was weak. I struggled. But today I have said YES! I am ready for your light to shine down upon me. I am no longer afraid of the dark. Here I am Jesus. YES, here I am! In Jesus' name, in Jesus' name, AMEN!

Building a Relationship with God

1. Begin praying at home
2. Find a place of worship (church)
3. Attend church weekly
4. Join a church ministry and participate monthly
5. Ask Jesus Christ his purpose for you
6. Accept Jesus Christ as your LORD and Savior

Now that you have read about ***Emotional Health***, continue reading onto Chapter 3 to learn of the challenges faced regarding ***Self-Identity*** and what the Holy Scripture revealed.

Related Scriptures

A glad heart makes a happy face; a broken heart crushes the spirit. **(Proverbs 15:13 NLT)**
Search me, O God, and know my heart; test me and know my anxious thoughts. **(Psalms 139:23 NLT)**
A cheerful heart is good medicine, but a broken spirit saps a person's strength. (**Proverbs 17:22 NLT)**
Those who plant in tears will harvest with shouts of *joy*. **(Psalms 126:5 NLT)**

Emotional Health Help Resources

https://www.samhsa.gov/data/report/2018-national-directory-mental-health-treatment-facilities (1-877-726-4727)
http://www.nacbt.org/contact-us/
https://www.apa.org/helpcenter/ (800) 374-2721)

Chapter 3

Self-Identity

Once you had no identity as a people; now you are God's people. Once you received no mercy; now you have received God's mercy. **(1 Peter 2:10 NLT)**

Imagine a world where you are accepted by peers. A world deprived of struggles to find your place in society. Ask yourself, "Am I living in such a world today?" If the answer is "Yes," you are one of the lucky few who experience such a luxury. For many, the answer is an awe-inspiring "No." In today's world, society influences us one way or the other to "self-identify." All around us, the added pressure to self-identify is apparent. From the moment we are born into this world until we leave it, we are involuntarily obligated to self-identify. These channels to self-identity include, but not limited to, sexual orientation, ethnicity, gender, race, age, sexual orientation, religion, social class, disability, culture, etc. It is a constant struggle to find your place in a society where you are faced with so many decisions deemed important.

Whether your decisions are perceived as easy or complex, we self-identify with our daily decision making. If I purchase and wear expensive shoes and clothing, do peers view me as cool? If I partake in bullying, does this make me look superior? Am I following the latest trends? Some people may not view these decision points as important. However, for you, it may be at the core of your daily decision-making process. And that is OK! Remember to remain true to yourself and your beliefs. *But the Holy Spirit produces this kind of fruit in our lives: love, joy, peace, patience, kindness, goodness, faithfulness* ***(Galatians 5:22 NLT)***.

Take a second to self-reflect and consider your answer to this question: **Who am I?** Let us continue for a moment. Choose ten words that describe your personality and write them down:

____

____

____

____

____

How challenging was it for you to find these ten words? Learning and coming to terms with the person you are can be an eye-opening life experience. Self-identity has many facets, and it requires effort on your part to continuously maneuver through them. How did you go about describing yourself? As a case in point, did you use descriptive words to include trustworthy, genuine, courageous, sincere, sensitive, and compassionate? There are no correct or incorrect responses in describing your personality. You were born an exceptional person and embracing your many facets is a significant step to self-identifying.

"Who you want to be is already inside of you waiting for you to confront who you are and tag them in to help you win the battle of the mind."

— Sanjo Jendayi

Source: https://www.goodreads.com/quotes/tag/self-identity

We live in a world with over 7 billion people and growing. By the year 2050, the population will be greater than 9 billion. You might ask: "Why are population growth numbers important to me?" The short answer is: *our society plays a massive, yet an important part in defining your self-identity.* The world we live in directly impacts the way we self-identify. As a youth, I had a creative personality. I had quite the imagination and still do this day. Part of defining my self-identity began with this personality trait. For you, it might be one of the following or many more not listed here:

Diplomatic (strategic, respectful, attentive, etc.) An example of attentiveness includes being absorbent when communicating. Asking questions and making eye contact.

Analytical (precise, focused, attention to detail, etc.) As a case in point, attention to detail is working on a school project while ensuring clear objectives and requirements are established. And every detailed step is hashed out to guarantee successful completion.

Empathetic (thoughtful, compassionate, sensitive, etc.) To illustrate, compassionate is being there for a friend who is experiencing adversity in his or her life. Listening to their concerns and providing reassurance of comfort to them.

Creative (artistic, imaginative, innovative, etc.) For instance, imaginative is deciding on your mode of approach to a problem or decision-point in your life. This is accomplished through focusing your mind and allowing creative thoughts to flow.

Regardless if any of the personality traits listed above applies to you, the key takeaway is that self-identity is an important definition (qualities, characteristics, or abilities) of who you are.

Let us reflect on what the Holy Scripture reveals: *Once you had no identity as a people; now you are God's people. Once you received no mercy; now you have received God's mercy* ***(1 Peter 2:10 NLT)***. What does the scripture mean by the phrase, *"Once you had no identity as a people; now you are Gods people?"*

The LORD is saying at some point in our lives we lose our identity. This means we wandered away from the word of Christ and down the path of imperfection. But there is no need to worry.

The LORD has got your back. Have you ever gazed into the mirror and did not recognize the person staring back in the reflection? Sometimes we forget the person we were because we are blinded by the person we have become. The LORD is calling out to you. He wants to place you on a new path to self-identity. The LORD did not say, *"Now you are God's people,"* without merit. He meant every word. When he died for us on the cross, we once again became his children cleansed of all sins. Let us focus on the second sentence of the Holy Scripture. *Once you received no mercy; now you have received God's mercy.* We, you, have all received the LORD's mercy through his sacrifice on the cross. The love he has for you is immeasurable, and God will help you overcome this daily life-struggle. You have received the LORD's mercy; take this moment to turn over a new page in your life. Use this new beginning to accept the Holy Spirit.

FOCUS ON THE PLAN God has set forth for you. Life circumstances have a unique way of derailing God's plans for you. Restoring your faith in him and focusing on his plan is the way to get back on the chosen path. No more shall the unforeseen circumstances in life cause you to lose sight of your true identity. In the days of uncertainty, allow your inner spirit to pull you closer to the LORD. Developing a spiritual dependence on the LORD falls in line with his plan for you. Nothing happens by chance in God's kingdom. Every outcome in his kingdom materializes into precise details set forth by the LORD. Instead of trying to analyze and conclude what he has in store for you, channel that energy into trust and belief.

Prepare Your Heart for the LORD's Prayer!

Let us pray: My LORD and savior Jesus Christ, thank you for this day. The day in which I have decided to put my struggle in your forgiving hands. The day in which I found strength and peace in my heart to let you take over my life and save me. Save me from my doubts. Save me from my inner voice of weakness. I accept you as my path to self-identity and everlasting life.

There was a time LORD I was lost and searching for an answer. And now I have found you, Jesus. I surrender my struggle to you. Knowing you are more than capable of turning my life around. There is no earthly struggle LORD that is too complicated for you. From this day forth, I will turn to you in time of struggle; in time of peace; in time of happiness; and in time of praise. What a day it is! The day you reached for my hand and led me down the road to redemption. In Jesus' name, in Jesus' name, AMEN!

Building a Relationship with God
1. Begin praying at home
2. Find a place of worship (church)
3. Attend church weekly
4. Join a church ministry and participate monthly
5. Ask Jesus Christ his purpose for you
6. Accept Jesus Christ as your LORD and Savior

Now that you have read about ***Self-Identity***, let us move onto the second section and begin reading Chapter 4 to learn of the challenges faced regarding ***Depression and Suicide*** and what the Holy Scripture revealed.

Related Scriptures

My people have been lost sheep. Their shepherds have led them astray and turned them loose in the mountains. They have lost their way and can't remember how to get back to the sheepfold. **(Jeremiah 50:6 NLT)**

If you look for me wholeheartedly, you will find me. **(Jeremiah 29:13 NLT)**

For whoever finds me finds life and receives favor from the Lord. **(Proverbs 8:35 NLT)**

I love all who love me. Those who search will surely find me. **(Proverbs 8:17 NLT)**

Self-Identity Help Resources

https://www.goodtherapy.org/learn-about-therapy/issues/identity-issues
1-888-563-2112 ext. 1
https://www.goodtherapy.org/contact-us.html
https://www.mirror-mirror.org/email.htm
https://www.mirror-mirror.org/identity-and-self-esteem.htm

SECTION II

CONQUERING YOUR FEARS AND TRIUMPH

In his unfailing love, my God will stand with me. He will let me look down in triumph on all my enemies. ***(Psalm 59:10 NLT)***

Chapter 4

Depression and Suicide

The LORD himself will fight for you. Just stay calm.
(*Exodus 14:14 NLT*)

Let us take a second to think about this chapter's title: *Depression and Suicide.*

Too many people including family, friends, coworkers, celebrities, church members, role models, etc., have all fought with this daily life-struggle. Whether past or present, we have heard of someone close or through media outlets of a celebrity losing the fight to depression and suicide. There is not a correct, incorrect, or easy way to touch on the lives lost. But it is time to stand up and shed light on the lives we can still save; even yours. Before we continue to reflect on this daily life-struggle, I need to express:

If you or anyone you know is experiencing depression and/or suicidal thoughts, please seek help immediately. Reach out to friends, family members, church ministry, personal prayer to Jesus Christ, a local physician, local or private health provider, a mental health specialist, etc. ***Take action!*** *Despite how dark and hopeless the world might seem, there are people who cares deeply about your well-being.*

"When you're surrounded by all these people, it can be lonelier than when you're by yourself. You can be in a huge crowd, but if you don't feel like you can trust anyone or talk to anybody, you feel like you're really alone."

— Fiona Apple

Source: https://sloganshub.org/depression-quotes/

Tens of millions of people around the globe have experienced or suffers from the inherited signs of depression. This epidemic affects our well-being and is accompanied by thoughts of suicide or ultimately, the act itself. Although depression is notoriously linked to suicide, other life stressors may contribute to this role. Other life stressors include substance abuse, mental and physical health, personal relationship problems, loss of immediate family, loss of social status, etc. Feeling of sadness or withdrawal from friends and family is way too familiar if you are going through this daily life-struggle. The key is to express how you are feeling to friends, family, healthcare provider, local church ministry, etc. Have you considered a short prayer to Jesus Christ asking for guidance? Here are some warning signs associated with depression and suicidal thoughts:

- *Mentioning to others you want to die or killing yourself*
- *Seeking ways to kill yourself*
- *Voicing to others, you are a burden or feeling trapped*
- *Increasing your alcohol and drug intake*
- *Expressing an increased level of anger or rage*
- *Demonstrating mood swings*
- *Having trouble sleeping*

- *A feeling of sadness, hopelessness, guilt, anxiousness*

There is nothing to be ashamed of. Take action and reach out to a person of trust or professional health organization and begin a conversation. You are not alone. There is hope. Reach out to professional organizations for help. See help resources at the end of this chapter and the end of this book made available to you or talk to someone you trust, i.e., friends, family members, local church ministry, etc. Depression is curable, and the sooner you seek and get help, the sooner you can be on your way to recovery and regaining control of your life. Keep fighting because the LORD is by your side. *He will once again fill your mouth with laughter and your lips with shouts of joy* ***(Job 8:21 NLT)***.

List examples of personality traits your friends, family, and/or love ones appreciate about you. Take a moment to consider and write them down.

____

____

____

____

____

Did you list personality traits comprising of confident, dependable, trusting, helpful, loyal, compassionate, etc.? Focus on the inherited life benefits of living without depression. Imagine friends and family once again having your love, warmth, joyous, and wonderful "you" again. A positive and new outlook on life will follow. Living freely without the struggles of depression lends itself to a happier life. Do not be hard on yourself and think positively.

Remain in positive thoughts and do not allow yourself to wander off to a place of negative thinking. Living this way may rob you of hope and quickly consume you. Practicing the compassionate gestures of kindness and love places you on an emotional path of positivity. The LORD believes in you and he will give you the strength to overcome and conquer this struggle. Just ask him!

Let us reflect on what the Holy Scripture reveals: *The LORD himself will fight for you. Just stay calm* ***(Exodus 14:14 NLT)***. What is the scripture referring to when it states, *"The LORD himself will fight for you?"* Let us examine further. The scripture relayed to you that whatever the obstacles you are facing. Whatever the circumstances. Jesus Christ will ensure you make it through. He will protect you against any foreseen or unforeseen circumstances headed your way. We may forget that the LORD is by our side daily. He never leaves us, and we should find comfort in knowing you have a proven warrior going into battle with you.

Take relaxation in knowing you are more than prepared to combat whatever comes your way when the LORD takes the lead. The second part of the scripture reads, *"Just stay calm."* This is easier said than done. Remaining calm during troubling times can be an uphill battle. This is where you need to develop "layered faith." Layered faith means you take baby steps as you encounter new and challenging obstacles. No one wakes up one day and says, "I have faith, and nothing can derail me." This is an ongoing faith-building exercise where you and Jesus Christ create a bond of faith through every struggle and triumph. As time passes, your faith will grow immensely and your ability to handle imminent challenges on your path is met by a better equipped you. There will always be new struggles in our lives, but we diminish the burden when you accept Jesus Christ as your savior. The LORD knows what you need or lack in your life. Therefore, he knows what is best for you.

TRUST IN EVERY ASPECT of the promise God made to you. Succumbing to self-assessments and evaluations of your present state only leads to frustration. Break the cycle of self-doubt through regular communication with the LORD. Develop a daily rhythm of prayer, patience, and faith. Through prayers, you have a loving Father who listens to your every concern and knows of a solution for you. Through patience, you have a Father who is hard at work in solving your daily life-struggle. Through faith, you have a Father who has already found a solution for you. Developing a daily rhythm leads to relationship building with the LORD.

Prepare Your Heart for the LORD's Prayer!

Let us pray: LORD, I have given life a second chance. I need your guidance from this day forth. Why? You are a proven savior, a proven warrior, a worthy father. Thank you for giving me the strength to overcome this challenge. When I fall short in understanding and faith, grant me discernment that I may get back on the right path to wisdom. Yesterday was rather challenging, but today is comforting. I found comfort in knowing I may rely on you during the good times, the easy times, the hard times, and all the days of my life. I pray that you help others in this world who are also experiencing this struggle, just as you did for me. Welcome them as they receive you in their lives as a token of hope. I ask that you fill my heart with the Holy Spirit and grant me the courage to begin a new page in my life. Oh, I am so excited to begin this lifelong journey with you! Here I am LORD. I am ready to commit my life to you. In Jesus' name, in Jesus' name, AMEN!

Building a Relationship with God

1. Begin praying at home
2. Find a place of worship (church)
3. Attend church weekly
4. Join a church ministry and participate monthly
5. Ask Jesus Christ his purpose for you
6. Accept Jesus Christ as your LORD and Savior

Now that you have read about ***Depression and Suicide***, continue reading onto Chapter 5 to learn of the challenges faced regarding ***Eating Disorder*** and what the Holy Scripture revealed.

Related Scriptures
As soon as I pray, you answer me; you encourage me by giving me strength. **(Psalms 138:3 NLT)** I pray that God, the source of hope, will fill you completely with joy and peace because you trust in him. Then you will overflow with confident hope through the power of the Holy Spirit. **(Romans 15:13 NLT)** I am very happy now because I have complete confidence in you. **(2 Corinthians 7:16 NLT)** Happy are those who hear the joyful call to worship, for they will walk in the light of your presence, Lord. **(Psalms 89:15 NLT)**

Depression and Suicide Help Resources
Suicide Prevention Hotline (1-800-827-7571) Suicide Hotline (1-800-SUICIDE) (784-2433) National Suicide Prevention Lifeline 1-800-273-TALK (8255) National Depression Association (1-800-826-3632)

Chapter 5

Eating Disorders

I have wandered away like a lost sheep; come and find me, for I have not forgotten your commands. ***(Psalm 119:176 NLT)***

Have you ever felt guilty or ashamed of the eating tendencies developed over the years? Have you used your body shape or weight to measure your self-esteem? Most people believe an eating disorder only involves over-eating. Does this assumption indicate if you devoured three servings of roasted turkey, sweet potato casserole, and pumpkin pie on Thanksgiving Day you have an eating disorder? Absolutely not! It probably means you have an appetite of a caveman. When was the last time you overate? How did it make you feel? Take a moment to consider and write how you felt.

____

____

____

____

____

Overeating, in this case, does not mean you have an eating disorder and could be summed up as an overindulgence of Thanksgiving Day feasts. For other people, excessive or inadequate food intake is all too real. The inherited effects of an eating disorder can negatively influence your life, everyone around you, and your overall well-being in unimaginable ways. Do not worry and have faith in the LORD. *Faith shows the reality of what we hope for; it is the evidence of things we cannot see* ***(Hebrews 11:1 NLT)***. Binge Eating Disorder, Bulimia Nervosa, and Anorexia Nervosa are some of the more common eating disorders. If you feel you have a case of an eating disorder, please seek medical consultation and regain your life.

"No two eating disorders are the same.

No two individuals are the same.

No two paths to recovery are the same.

But everyone's strength to reach recovery IS the same."

— Brittany Burgunder

Source: https://www.goodreads.com/quotes/9096366-no-two-eating-disorders-are-the-same-no-two-individuals

---

The first eating disorder is *Binge Eating.* This is an epidemic affecting many people. Although treatable, this disorder inflicts havoc and makes it a daily struggle for anyone experiencing the heartache of limiting their daily food intake. If you partake in Binge Eating, there is a high probability of becoming obese stemming from adverse weight gain. As a case in point, a person who regularly partakes in overeating is at great risk of becoming obese. As a result, a feeling of guilt is experienced and may spiral into depression. This person needs immediate professional assistance to help overcome the urges of binge eating.

(*Source: https://www.eatingdisorderfoundation.org/learn-more/about-eating-disorders/*)

The second eating disorder is *Bulimia Nervosa.* This eating disorder steals your joy of living a normal life. A person experiencing Bulimia Nervosa overeats and immediately regurgitates his or her meal as a corrective measure. Dealing with Bulimia Nervosa is a serious matter and the realities of the struggle. Repeatedly, partaking in binge eating and immediately vomiting is all too familiar. People do this because they feel eating results in immediate weight gain and a negative change in their body shape. By way of illustration, a person might overeat during a luncheon only to turn around and vomit because the feeling of guilt kicked in.

(*Source: https://www.eatingdisorderfoundation.org/learn-more/about-eating-disorders/*)

And the third eating disorder is *Anorexia Nervosa.* This eating disorder affects the mindset of everyone believing they are overweight. This is far from the truth and forces a person to live in a constant state of fear because of the perception of being overweight. This fear forces an individual to deliberately strive to subconsciously maintain an otherwise unhealthy body weight. For instance, a person might look normal according to friends, colleagues, and family. However, when that person looks into the mirror, they perceive themselves as being overweight.

(Source: https://www.eatingdisorderfoundation.org/learn-more/about-eating-disorders/)

Let us reflect on what the Holy Scripture reveals: *I have wandered away like a lost sheep; come and find me, for I have not forgotten your commands* **(Psalm 119:176 NLT)**. The scripture reads, *"I have wandered away like a lost sheep."* We tend to lose focus on the Holy Scripture and the intent of the LORD's message for us. When the scripture refers to us as a *lost sheep*, it is simply stating we lost track of the LORD's message and it is time for us to return to him. As a similar point, a person might have attended church consistently, traveled on missionary trips around the world, and performed the LORD's deeds. However, over time that person was confronted with a life-changing event and this event drastically altered the course of his or her life.

Disappointingly, he or she lost what they held of value with the LORD. His purpose for them. Jesus Christ said, *"Come and find me."* This means to turn your life around and focus on him. He awaits you and it is easy to find him. Find him through prayer. Ask Jesus Christ to place you once again on the path to everlasting life. Refocus on his purpose for you. The LORD did not forget his purpose for you. The scripture read, *"For I have not forgotten your commands."* The commands were established to keep you on track and in favor with the LORD. He wants you to follow his commands and return to good standings with him. He has not forgotten your commands, and neither should you. How do you accomplish this? Find time daily to read the Holy Bible and reflect on the LORD's message through a reflection of the scriptures. Ask God to grant you discernment of the scriptures, so you can understand its message. Attend your local church ministry and ask how you can follow the LORD's commands.

LIVING ONE DAY at a time with the LORD. Practicing this daily keeps you in close relations with the LORD. Self-doubt is a natural response, especially when you lived many days in fear of dealing with an eating disorder. Learn to trust God in all circumstances and know the favorable outcome to your struggle is not short-lived, but everlasting. Channel your energy to the LORD's promise for his children. His promise of a joyous life. The misconception of a worry-free life does not exist. Human nature is to worry about life's uncertainties because we strive to be in control of every aspect and outcome. You might roll the dice, but the LORD decides each outcome.

Prepare Your Heart for the LORD's Prayer!

Let us pray: Heavenly Father, I am taking a hard stance and decided to change my life behaviors. I am changing my attitude towards eating disorders. I understand this disorder has impacted my family, friends, and loved ones. It is time LORD for me to become more courageous than ever. Thank you for remaining patient with me. Thank you for listening to my call for help. I need your guidance and help to jump over this hurdle placed before me. I believe in your promise of love and care for your children, me. I am tired of wrestling with this struggle. I need your strength LORD to endure, recover, and persevere.

Please guide me in the right direction and enable me to make the life changes to overcome this struggle. I promise LORD from this day forth, my trust in you will grow stronger because of your willingness to show me a resolution to this struggle. I pray for the day when I can live a life without an eating disorder impacting my outlook. I am so fortunate to have a loving Father like you who will always be there to comfort me. I am proud to have a God who is so forgiving and understanding of my life blunders. Where would I be if it were not for you LORD? You have been my cloud of comfort; my foundational rock; and my knight in battle. Thank you, LORD. In Jesus' name, in Jesus' name, AMEN!

Building a Relationship with God
1. Begin praying at home
2. Find a place of worship (church)
3. Attend church weekly
4. Join a church ministry and participate monthly
5. Ask Jesus Christ his purpose for you
6. Accept Jesus Christ as your LORD and Savior

Now that you have read about ***Eating Disorder***, continue reading onto Chapter 6 to learn of the challenges faced regarding ***Teen Pregnancy*** and what the Holy Scripture revealed.

Related Scriptures

This hope is a strong and trustworthy anchor for our souls. It leads us through the curtain into God's inner sanctuary. **(Hebrews 6:19 NLT)**

So be strong and courageous, all you who put your hope in the Lord. **(Psalms 31:24 NLT)**

Rejoice in our confident hope. Be patient in trouble and keep on praying. **(Romans 12:12 NLT)**

Yes, there are many parts, but only one body. **(1 Corinthians 12:20 NLT)**

Eating Disorder Help Resources

Eating Disorders Awareness and Prevention (1-800-931-2237)

Eating Disorders Center (1-888-236-1188)

National Association of Anorexia Nervosa and Associated Disorders (1-847-831-3438)

Chapter 6

Teen Pregnancy

Send me a sign of your favor. Then those who hate me will be put to shame, for you, O LORD, help and comfort me. ***(Psalm 86:17 NLT)***

There are many teenagers under the age of eighteen who are parents or soon to become parents of children. If you are considering becoming a teen parent … WAIT! I AM NOT AN ADVOCATE FOR TEEN PREGNANCY. I can hardly imagine how difficult it may feel to deal with such an important responsibility. In truth, you are not too far removed from being a child yourself. Parenting is challenging and unpredictable. In the perfect world, most adults take the time to plan for a family. Adults choose the right partner to settle down with and begin a family. But what if you did not plan to become pregnant?

Experimenting with premarital sex may come with life-changing responsibilities. I remembered my father stating to me, "If you become pregnant at a young age, it will be difficult to finish school and get a good-paying job." Perhaps my chances of succeeding in life would diminish entirely. My father's statement made me consider the consequences of teen pregnancy. How do I balance future goals and parenting? I contemplated the unknown and decided that becoming a teen parent was not in the best interest of my future. What are your future goals in life? How would you balance parenting and pursuance of future goals? Take a moment to consider and write your response.

____

____

____

____

____

I do not believe my father made an accurate statement completely. Here is why. There are millions of teen parents in this world who overcame the challenges of being a young parent and moved on in life to become successful. *Don't let anyone think less of you because you are young. Be an example to all believers in what you say, in the way you live, in your love, your faith, and your purity* ***(1 Timothy 4:12 NLT)***. Do you want to know the truth about the statement my father made many years ago? *Difficult*. This is the truth about the statement. It is difficult to become pregnant as a youth, attend school, and/or pursue a career simultaneously.

This is immensely challenging, however possible. While many factors come into play and obstacles placed on your path, it can be accomplished. Having a reliable support system, including family and friends, is always helpful. If you are pregnant, it is very important to care for yourself and your baby. This includes regularly visiting a medical doctor for prenatal care. Stay away from harmful habits like drugs and alcohol. Remember to avoid smoking, both first and second hand. If you partake in sexual activities while pregnant, use protection.

"Babies are bits of star-dust blown from the hand of God. Lucky is the woman who knows the pangs of birth for she has held a star."

— Larry Barretto

Source: https://www.sermoncentral.com/sermon-illustrations/57818/babies-are-bits-of-stardust-blown-from-the-hand-by-sermoncentral

---

We know how important it is to ensure young parents receive adequate academic, emotional, and medical support for themselves and the child's future. I have included some helpful points of contact in the Help Resources section. The birth of a child is joyous. However, careful planning is essential to successful parenting.

Focus on the future. Take this opportunity to push forward in life. A baby is not a reason to lose focus on your future. For instance, if you aspire to become a lawyer, doctor, or a different career of choice, the opportunity is still in reach. All you need to do is refocus. Focus on your dreams and hold on to them. Although it may become difficult, you are more than capable of achieving anything you want in life. Hold your head up and keep moving forward.

Find a support system. Reach out to family, friends, local church ministry, etc. to receive support. Other parents have gone through similar experiences and possess the wisdom and knowledge to share with you. To illustrate, a support system may enable you to find the required time to attend school, work more hours on the job, or advise on how to become a better parent.

Find personal time for yourself. Although you are overwhelmed with being a parent, it is essential to find your "me time." Setting aside a few minutes for quiet time to refresh and re-energize your mind and body is important to staying on track and moving forward in life. "Me time" is spent doing activities you like doing. For example, if you like to read, make the time. The conceived notion is when you do activities that make you happy; you approach life challenges with a positive attitude. I believe in you!

Let us reflect on what the Holy Scripture reveals: *Send me a sign of your favor. Then those who hate me will be put to shame, for you, O LORD, help and comfort me* ***(Psalm 86:17 NLT)***. Let us start by paying close attention to what the scripture states. "*Send me a sign of your favor.*" Not because you are pregnant means you are out of favor with the LORD. The LORD wants you to move closer to him during this challenging time and ask for his support. Yes. He wants you to reach out through prayer and ask him for courage, faith, and resolution.

Knowing the LORD is just a short prayer away from intervening, do not delay. When you communicate through prayer, let him know how you feel at that very moment and ask him to show you the way. The second part of the scripture reads, "*Then those who hate me will be put to shame.*" What if you are experiencing or feeling a lack of support from close friends or family members? If so, then you probably feel like the world itself has turned away from you. The LORD is reminding you that whoever is criticizing or pointing fingers, will be held accountable.

The LORD does not approve of his children passing judgment against each other. He loves when his children express support during challenging times. The last part of the scripture alluded to the LORD providing *help and comfort*. As you go through this daily life-struggle, remember the LORD is there with you through thick and thin. The challenges you face today prepare you for the ones to come.

DO NOT BE AFRAID of the unknown. Your inability to see into the future is an opportunity for dependency on the

LORD. The blind might lack sight, but the blind has an abundant vision. This means walking by faith and not by sight is a practice of the Godly. You do not need sight to see the LORD's favorable outcomes for your daily life-struggle of teen pregnancy. Rather, believe in his plan for you. When you confide in the LORD, a bond of trust is created. Turning to him daily for resolutions to your uncertainties leads to a layer of faith that is unbreakable. Instead of battling problems on your own, concentrate on trusting the LORD. Remember the LORD is your song of joy. Whisper his name during quiet times. Shout his name during worship. And, seek his name during times of uncertainty.

Prepare Your Heart for the LORD's Prayer!

Let us pray: Heavenly Father, please lead me through this time of uncertainty. The road I am about to travel is dark and filled with doubts. I ask you to be my light of hope. This journey is an entanglement of excitement and nervousness. Let your blessings of hope shine down upon me. How can I express my gratitude to you, LORD? The gratitude of knowing you are here with me. I want to say Thank You! I understand my child is a blessing from you. Whenever I feel overwhelmed, I will look to you for direction. I am blessed to have you as my LORD and

Savior. Yes, on this day and all the days forth, I will follow your direction. I am a believer LORD. I believe in your power and grace. I believe you are the highest God. I pray thy will be done and may you bless me and my child. Take me by the hand and lead me to victory. In Jesus' name, in Jesus' name, AMEN!

Building a Relationship with God
1. Begin praying at home
2. Find a place of worship (church)
3. Attend church weekly
4. Join a church ministry and participate monthly
5. Ask Jesus Christ his purpose for you
6. Accept Jesus Christ as your LORD and Savior

Now that you have read about ***Teen Pregnancy***, continue reading onto Chapter 7 to learn of the challenges faced regarding ***Single-Parent Households*** and what the Holy Scripture revealed.

Related Scriptures

You have given me your shield of victory. Your right hand supports me; your help has made me great.
(Psalms 18:35 NLT)
I wait quietly before God, for my victory comes from him.
(Psalms 62:1 NLT)
I thank you for answering my prayer and giving me victory. **(Psalms 118:21 NLT)**
For the Lord delights in his people; he crowns the humble with victory. **(Psalms 149:4 NLT)**

Teen Pregnancy Help Resources

American Pregnancy Association (1-800-672-2296)
American Pregnancy Association (1-800-672-2296)
Planned Parenthood Federation of America (1-800-230-PLAN)
Crisis Call Center (1-800-273-8255) or text ANSWER to 839863

Chapter 7

Single-Parent Households

Grandchildren are the crowning glory of the aged; parents are the pride of their children. ***(Proverbs 17:6 NLT)***

I have a confession. I was raised in a single-parent household. For children growing up in this environment, there are inherited advantages and disadvantages. The disadvantages include:

1) *Problems adjusting to new relationships.* Children may experience a difficult time adjusting to and accepting any potential stepparent. A child may simply do not want to split personal time with a potential stepparent.

2) *Negative feelings toward parents.* Children may feel this way because they do not understand why both parents failed to make the relationship work.

3) *Financial struggles.* Financial hardship is the reality of a single-parent household. There is not enough money to pay for items outside of daily necessities.

4) *Loss of quality time.* As a youth, the main concern is whether the quality time is available to share as a new stepparent comes into the picture.

The advantages of having and accepting a new stepparent may change your outlook. The advantages include:

1) *A feeling of closeness.* Transitioning from having one parent to both in the household creates a feeling of closeness and a display of unity from both parents.

2) *A sense of structure.* Now that you have both supporting cast members in the household, this allows for a community of structure where you have two outlets to voice your concerns and issues.

3) *Stability.* Where both parents are concerned, they can provide you with the stability that you lacked before.

4) *Financial liberty.* Having two incomes in the household allows for greater financial freedom to pay expenses and the ability to afford more leisure activities.

"Single moms: You are a doctor, a teacher, a nurse, a maid, a cook, a referee, a heroine, a provider, a defender, a protector, a true Superwoman. Wear your cape proudly."

— Mandy Hale

Source: https://www.goodreads.com/quotes/861876-single-moms-you-are-a-doctor-a-teacher-a-nurse

---

What do you think are some advantages and disadvantages of single-parent households? Take a moment to consider and write them down.

____

____

____

____

____

Life has dealt us certain cards, and it is up to us in overcoming the odds. Place your trust in Jesus Christ, and he will see you through. *Yes, the Lord has done amazing things for us! What joy!* **(*Psalms 126:3 NLT*)**. I am not an advocate for single-parent households, nor is it the best way for a child to be raised. I believe children should be raised in a loving home with both parents commonly referred to as a "nuclear family." A nuclear family consists of a father, mother, and child. But what if this is not the reality for you? What if one parent is not there in your life? Most people believe single-parent households involve one parent choosing to be absent from the child's life. This is a vague assumption and far from the reality children live today.

There are many contributing factors to single-parent households, including incarceration, the passing of a parent, military assignment, financial instability, drug addiction, unmarried parents, divorce, etc. Single-parent households are more common today. We are no longer surprised to witness single fathers, single mothers, grandparents, or older siblings being the head of household. There is also the consensus that growing up in a single-parent household is significantly more stressful for everyone involved. We should not overlook what single parents must endure and overcome under these circumstances. There are many daily-unrealistic expectations single parents tackle, including maintaining or keeping a job, staying atop of household chores, paying household bills, tending to the needs of the child/children, developing or maintaining personal friendships, finding alone time, etc.

These are stressful times for single parents. What about the child/children? What about you? Children deal with many ramifications stemming from living in a single-parent household. As an example, what if your parents are separated, divorced, or never married? Arguments and conflicts between parents can add significant stress to your life. How about spending less time with your parents because they are too busy working to keep a roof over your head? What about trying to adjust to problems stemming from your parents starting a new relationship through dating? I remembered when my parents started dating as a youth. It was awful! I did not want to or liked the idea of a "stranger" stealing personal time away from us. Have you experienced this?

The life lesson I learned from not wanting to share personal time was "selfishness". It was selfish to automatically assume that the person would steal our personal time. I can attest that not all stepparents are bad, and they deserve an opportunity to prove it. The way you were raised shapes you into the person you are today.

While there are advantages and disadvantages to being raised in a single-parent household, the most important factor to remember is that you are more than capable of rising above it all.

Let us reflect on what the Holy Scripture reveals: *Grandchildren are the crowning glory of the aged; parents are the pride of their children* ***(Proverbs 17:6 NLT)***. Parents are proud to raise their children into responsible and loving adults. They are even more proud when those children begin a family of their own. As the scripture reads, *"Grandchildren are the crowning glory of the aged."* This can be interpreted in many ways. However, it is quite simple. When we become grandparents, it is a significant achievement of a lifetime. This means we are blessed to witness our grandchildren's arrival into this world. They are truly the crowning glory.

The second part of the scripture reads, *"Parents are the pride of their children."* Children should be proud to have parents in their lives. To have both parents in your life is a true blessing and should not be overlooked or taken for granted. The scripture revealed to us the family life cycle where you have three generations alive simultaneously. Grandparent, parent, and child.

ASK FOR UNDERSTANDING from Jesus Christ. In doing so, your eyes will be opened to witnessing the truth. Who else other than Jesus Christ that truly knows you better? There are no areas or aspects of your life he is not in tune with. He views your life with forgiveness, therefore do not feel ashamed. Allow his grace to shine down upon you, cleansing you of doubts. The journey of single-parent households is hard and challenging. When no one understands you and the challenges you are faced with, turn to him. Delight in knowing your God is a whisper away. Speak his name and he shall answer your calling. Who else understands your thoughts and understands your every desire? Allow him to cleanse you and refresh your outlook on life. Our LORD and Savior, Jesus Christ is an overflowing well of love, forgiveness, and understanding.

Prepare Your Heart for the LORD's Prayer!

Let us pray: Thank you, Jesus Christ, for this blessed day. I am so privileged to be in your presence of worship. Although I live in a single-parent household, I am surrounded by your loving grace. I know my worries are soon taken away because of your promise to me. The promise of direction along this journey. No matter the circumstances, you are far greater. Overcoming this struggle will become to pass. Please show me a sign of your favor.

Thank you, LORD. Thank you for this opportunity to be in your presence today. There is nowhere else I want to be than here in your comfort. As the sun rises tomorrow, so will my love for you. My faith will shine brighter because of this newfound hope. I am tired and weary of taking on this struggle alone. From this day forth, I will place it in your mighty hands. I am honored to accept you as my LORD. May your name be hailed across all seas and above all mountains, so the world may learn of the mighty and great Father you are to your children. In Jesus' name, in Jesus' name, AMEN!

Building a Relationship with God

1. Begin praying at home
2. Find a place of worship (church)
3. Attend church weekly
4. Join a church ministry and participate monthly
5. Ask Jesus Christ his purpose for you
6. Accept Jesus Christ as your LORD and Savior

Now that you have read about ***Single-Parent Households***, let us move onto the third section and begin reading Chapter 8 to learn of the challenges faced regarding ***Child Abuse*** and what the Holy Scripture revealed.

Related Scriptures
Since God chose you to be the Holy People he loves, you must clothe yourselves with tenderhearted mercy, kindness, humility, gentleness, and patience. **(Colossians 3:12 NLT)** I know all the things you do. I have seen your love, your faith, your service, and your patient endurance. And I can see your constant improvement in all these things. **(Revelation 2:19 NLT)** A tree is identified by its fruit. If a tree is good, its fruit will be good. If a tree is bad, its fruit will be bad. **(Matthew 12:33 NLT)** Patient endurance is what you need now, so that you will continue to do God's will. Then you will receive all that he has promised. **(Hebrews 10:36 NLT)**

Single-Parent Households Help Resources
http://www.singlemoms.org/housing-resources-for-single-mothers/ National Parent Helpline (1-855-427-2736) https://singlemothersgrants.org/tanf-cash-assistance-for-single-mothers/

SECTION III

YOU ARE NOT ALONE

The LORD your God is going ahead of you. He will fight for you, just as you saw him do in Egypt. ***(Deuteronomy 1:30 NLT)***

Chapter 8

Child Abuse

Do not touch my chosen people, and do not hurt my prophets. ***(1 Chronicles 16:22 NLT)***

Parents find themselves disciplining children of their own. The ways of administering discipline may result in child abuse. Regardless if a parent uses physical or verbal means, the opportunity presents itself to cause harm to a child. Has your parent(s) gone overboard and caused you emotional or physical harm? You should not be exposed to either. Legal troubles could be an immediate ramification for a parent who causes hurt to a child. If you were/are a victim, then you are all too familiar with the rage or anger dished out by mom, dad, other family members, etc. This is a frustrating and sensitive issue. Child abuse causes a lasting reminder of emotional and physical wounds. Parents must learn of the long-term damaging effects placed on a child. Sometimes parents find it hard to restrain from causing harm because of anger. Administering discipline while experiencing anger is an unwise decision.

"Childhood should be carefree, playing in the sun; not living a nightmare in the darkness of the soul."

— Dave Pelzer, A Child Called "It"

Source: https://www.goodreads.com/quotes/225456-childhood-should-be-carefree-playing-in-the-sun-not-living

---

Parents need to take a moment and calm down. Remain calm while disciplining your children to avoid physical or emotional harm. What if this child is you? Child abuse is known to have many forms. Sexual, physical, exploitation, neglect, and emotional are some forms of abuse. Increasing your awareness of this epidemic is the first step toward making a positive change. Emotional abuse is harmful in numerous ways. For instance, parents are responsible for raising a child to become strong independent adults. What happens when a child does not live up to mom's or dad's expectations? Some parents may feel the need to lash out by yelling or screaming while enraged. This action can cause long-term emotional trauma and should be avoided at all costs.

Communicating your displeasure in a firm and caring manner provides reassurance of your love for them. The same can be said for physical abuse. Administering discipline while enraged is a dangerous act and once again should be avoided. For instance, striking with an object to administer discipline results in physical harm. Parents need to communicate when calm to avoid unintended consequences. A victim of unintended consequences may develop lifelong emotional scars. Children learn from their own experiences. Child abuse can have generational ramifications if the cycle is not broken. Children who are abused might continue this trend. Administering discipline, the way Mom or Dad once did.

Children may unconsciously learn from parents and use the same methods. These forms of abuse are passed down through generations until the cycle is broken. I call on you, "parents" to break this cycle. How do you think the cycle can be broken? Take a moment to consider and write your response.

____

____

____

____

____

The first step to emotional or physical healing is to remove one's self from the toxic environment and receive professional help. This step is easier said than done and requires tremendous courage to say, "Enough!" What if you are a minor and cannot remove yourself from this toxic environment? *Dear brothers and sisters, when troubles of any kind come your way, consider it an opportunity for great joy* ***(James 1:2 NLT)***.

Notifying other family members, school faculty, friends, or the authorities could be the deciding factor between emotional and physical trauma if you are a minor and unable to remove yourself from the situation. If you are a parent committing child abuse, I urge you to take a moment and talk with your child. Talking with your child regarding what he or she has done creates a positive environment and reinforces your love for them.

Let us reflect on what the Holy Scripture reveals: *Do not touch my chosen people, and do not hurt my prophets* ***(1 Chronicles 16:22 NLT).*** These are powerful words directed at us through scripture. "*Do not touch my chosen people.*" This is a direct warning from our Father. If you have ill intent, he is saying to stay away from his chosen people. How do we know who are God's chosen people? We cannot be 100% sure who these chosen people are. It could be a homeless person asking for help. It could be an ordained person leading a church. It could be you. You never know who God's prophets are, so why take a chance of offending him. The greater meaning behind this scripture is for us to treat everyone with love, not hatred. Imagine a world where you love everyone regardless of social class.

The second part of the scripture reads, "*Do not hurt my prophets.*" The LORD is saying to us; do not hurt them. Not sexually, physically, emotionally, through exploitation, abandonment, etc. He will tolerate none of it. Whether or not we are 100% sure, God chooses some of us to do his work here on earth. And because of that, the LORD will protect his children at all costs.

LEARN TO LIVE in peace and renounce all acts of mistreatment. The world is filled with trouble and despair. Who else but the LORD is more qualified to help you navigate through and around every corner? Allow him to fill you with his Holy Spirit and equip you with the tools needed to face the unrelenting flow of problems. The more faith you place in the LORD, the more capable you are of learning how to overcome daily life-struggles. There is no need to face struggles on your own. The LORD has the solutions and ready to share with you the path to a viable resolution. Whenever you find yourself worrying about a solution to child abuse, focus your thoughts on him. Communicate your thoughts and concerns to the LORD, and he will show you a way through.

Prepare Your Heart for the LORD's Prayer!

Let us pray: My LORD, thank you for reassuring me of your love. The reassured love that breaks down walls and conquers impenetrable hearts. You are a powerful God. Please come into my life and purify my heart. Enable me to see your graceful ways. Protect me from whoever attempts to emotionally and physically abuse me. Keep me safe in your caring hands. You are my champion through challenging moments of uncertainty.

I ask for your strength and courage that I may overcome what I am experiencing this day. I pray for those who caused me harm. I pray they realize the hurt they caused and repent all sins to you, LORD. Forgive them of their sins and wrongdoing. I pray that I forgive them as well. Allow me to overcome this moment and rise above it. Allow me to steer away from abusing my children when I become a parent. Enable me, LORD, to teach them the disadvantages of child abuse. In Jesus' name, in Jesus' name, AMEN!

Building a Relationship with God

1. Begin praying at home
2. Find a place of worship (church)
3. Attend church weekly
4. Join a church ministry and participate monthly
5. Ask Jesus Christ his purpose for you
6. Accept Jesus Christ as your LORD and Savior

Now that you have read about ***Child Abuse***, continue reading onto Chapter 9 to learn of the challenges faced regarding ***Bullying*** and what the Holy Scripture revealed.

Related Scriptures

Always be humble and gentle. Be patient with each other, making allowance for each other's faults because of your love. **(Ephesians 4:2 NLT)**

We put our hope in the Lord. He is our help and our shield. **(Psalms 33:20 NLT)**

The Lord is good to those who depend on him, to those who search for him. **(Lamentations 3:25 NLT)**

We can rejoice, too, when we run into problems and trials, for we know that they help us develop endurance. **(Romans 5:3 NLT)**

Child Abuse Help Resources

National Sexual Assault Hotline (1-800-656-HOPE (4673)
National Child Abuse Hotline (1-800-4-A-CHILD (422-4453)
Child Abuse Hotline / Dept of Social Services (1-800-342-3720)
Child Abuse National Hotline (1-800-25ABUSE)
Children in immediate danger (1-800-THE-LOST)
Exploitation of Children (1-800-843-5678)

Chapter 9

Bullying

LORD, you know the hopes of the helpless. Surely you will hear their cries and comfort them. ***(Psalm 10:17 NLT)***

Reminiscing on the days as a child fills my mind with joyous memories. I remembered running around on the school's playground on cool breezy days with no care about tomorrow. Although many days as a child brought smiles and laughter, I feared the days when much older and larger-sized children picked on me. I did not enjoy playing outside during school recess because of the fear. Those days were my first encounter of being a victim of bullying. I learned quickly that fighting bullies were not the best approach to a long-term solution. The fighting resulted in being on the receiving end of an emotional and physical bruising. And "bruising" is the best way to sum up what happened on the school's playground.

An intervention of the school's teacher was the better solution. The teacher repeatedly sat us down and we would discuss the issues in hope of a resolution. The intervention helped the situation greatly. The bully was not aware of the emotional and physical pain being inflicted. We all learned to bully was wrong. The harsh reality is that if you are a bully, people do not want to associate themselves with you. No one likes to be bullied. If you are a bully, change your approach to how you treat others and people will want to associate themselves with you. Bullying pushes people away and the best approach is to stop it.

"One's dignity may be assaulted, vandalized and cruelly mocked, but it can never be taken away unless it is surrendered."

— Michael J. Fox

Source: https://www.goodreads.com/quotes/195663-one-s-dignity-may-be-assaulted-vandalized-and-cruelly-mocked-but

---

A colleague of mine came up with a personal solution to bullying. The colleague implemented reversed psychology. As a case in point, while my colleague was being bullied, he asked the bully sarcastically if he wanted to become friends instead. Perplexing as it appeared, the bully agreed, and they became friends. Why? Bullies rarely have many friends, if any.

This scenario implied that the bully felt like an outcast and wanted a feeling of belonging. The bully's action was a cry for attention and help. There are many ways to approach and resolve bullying. The technique I shared was a previous life experience and may or may not work for you as it did for my colleague. Have you experienced bullying? Are you in fear of living your life being a victim of bullying?

Bullying is one of the cruelest problems facing our youth, and it affects millions just like you. "**Speak up to stand up!**" Speak up if you are a witness to bullying! *There is joy for those who deal justly with others and always do what is right* ***(Psalms 106:3 NLT)***. The ramifications of bullying causes fear and adversely impact your daily life. The absolute fact regarding bullying is that our youth live in a constant state of fear because of it. Long-term emotional effects, suicide, and depression are resulting ramifications.

Bullies tend to focus on the social status and appearance of the bullied. Verbal, social, and physical attacks are the most preferred methods for a bully. Verbal attacks come in the form of insults while physical attacks take the shape of an assault. Social attacks tend to stem from false rumors or intentionally trying to shame the bullied. What makes a child become a bully? Children that participate in bullying love the feeling of power they gain from establishing a sense of superiority over the bullied. A sense of superiority by a bully is achieved through physical strength or hurtful words. What do you think are the reasons people participate in bullying? Take a moment to consider and write your response.

____

____

____

____

____

In today's technological society, cyberbullying is another method used by bullies to cause mental trauma. This is impactful to the youth in real life, although this form of bullying is carried out virtually. Even though this method is conducted through voice messages, text messages, instant messages, emails, social media, etc., the bully's intent is still cruel and hurtful. If you partake in bullying, please stop.

They have linked bullying to more violent behaviors in adulthood. Once a bully reaches adulthood, the behavior negatively impacts his or her ability to fit into societal norms. The consequences of this behavior may lead to lost friendships, legal trouble, peer rejection, a sense of non-belonging, and even depression. If you are a witness or victim of bullying, speak up! Inform friends, family members, teachers, authorities, supervisors, church ministry, etc. There is no need to tolerate this behavior or subject yourself to its harshness.

One of the many ways of preventing bullying as an adult is to educate your children. Help them to understand bullying is cruel and teach them how to stand up safely to it. Children need to understand bullying is unacceptable on all levels. *Parents*: Speak with your children often. Keep the lines of communication open to learning about their everyday life events. Learn about your children's concerns and encourage them to say no to bullying.

Children: Do what you love and have fun. Participate in activities you love and treat each other with respect and compassion. If you are not experiencing the best of moods, do not take it out on others through verbal or physical means. Instead, communicate your issue(s) through a support-structure of trusted peers or adults. If you are a bully, it is not too late to reach out to a support group (friends, family members, teachers, supervisors, church ministry, etc.) for help. Bullying is a choice. Try to show respect for others. And, they will respect you.

Let us reflect on what the Holy Scripture reveals: *LORD, you know the hopes of the helpless. Surely you will hear their cries and comfort them* ***(Psalm 10:17 NLT)***. Experiencing bullying in school or virtually is not the only platform. By way of illustration, throughout history bullying took the form of oppressors stealing from the poor or dominant military forces conquering lesser nations. History revealed to us that the rich stole from the poor and powerful nations overpowered lesser nations.

The LORD *knows the hopes of the helpless.* He knows the bullied, his children, are crying out to him for relief from the anguish of fear and frustration. The scripture refers to his children as helpless. Rest assured, the LORD takes care of the helpless. He will find a solution for you. But he requires two things from you to accomplish this. First, the LORD wants you to ask him for help. And second, he wants you to have faith that he will help you through this issue.

The latter part of the scripture reads, *"Surely you will hear their cries and comfort them."* The LORD heard your cry for help, and he is working on a solution for you. He needs you to ask him through prayer. The term *comfort* implies that when you are facing difficult times, communicating through prayer offers a level of comfort because the LORD is listening to your cry for help.

EACH STEP CLOSER to God is a step closer towards spiritual growth. As you travel throughout the day with uncertainties and a loss for direction, the opportunity presents itself to grasp his mighty hands. Through your beliefs and dependencies in him, allow him the opportunity to take the lead and guide you throughout the day. Placing your concerns into the LORD's hands is a wise decision. He will provide to you a future deprived of living in fear of bullying. Whenever your thoughts wander off contemplating about bullying and the negative effects on your well-being, fixate your thoughts on the LORD. Turn to Him for comfort and peace. Practicing these daily builds trust between you and him. Rest assured, each step closer to him is accompanied by knowledge and understanding of your situation.

Prepare Your Heart for the LORD's Prayer!

Let us pray: LORD, I am here in your presence in need of intervention. I wish bullying did not affect me. I wish bullying would just disappear. This is a problem I am tired of facing alone. I ask for your guidance, your peace, your empathy. Show me a better way to confront my fear of bullying. I place my trust and faith in you, LORD. Grant me the courage to forgive my offenders and grant them wisdom to understand their wrongdoings. I pray for emotional healing and spiritual growth that I may regain what they took during this experience, self-confidence. I pray for the day when I can happily live without fear of bullying ever again. In Jesus' name, in Jesus' name, AMEN!

Building a Relationship with God

1. Begin praying at home
2. Find a place of worship (church)
3. Attend church weekly
4. Join a church ministry and participate monthly
5. Ask Jesus Christ his purpose for you
6. Accept Jesus Christ as your LORD and Savior

Now that you have read about ***Bullying***, continue reading onto Chapter 10 to learn of the challenges faced regarding ***Peer and Parental Pressure*** and what the Holy Scripture revealed.

Related Scriptures

The generous will prosper; those who refresh others will themselves be refreshed. **(Proverbs 11:25 NLT)**

May God, who gives this patience and encouragement, help you live in complete harmony with each other, as is fitting for followers of Christ Jesus. **(Romans 15:5 NLT)**

I waited patiently for the Lord to help me, and he turned to me and heard my cry. **(Psalms 40:1 NLT)**

Control your temper, for anger labels you a fool. **(Ecclesiastes 7:9 NLT)**

Bullying Help Resources

https://www.stopbullying.gov/

Cyber Bullying (1-800-829-0067)

https://www.stopbullying.gov/get-help-now/index.html

Chapter 10

Peer and Parental Pressure

As pressure and stress bear down on me, I find joy in your commands. **(Psalm 119:143 NLT)**

P*eer Pressure.* The role peer pressure plays in influencing our youth is enormous. Peer pressure influences us to make decisions outside of our comfort zone and may lead to life regrets. A life regret may stem from skipping class or school. The consequences of these actions may result in a lack of adequate education or an inability to obtain a professional career. Another life regret may come from partaking in illegal drugs. The consequences may result in drug addiction, incarceration, etc. Gaining popularity or acceptance by peers are two illustrations of life-decisions influencing our youth. The fear of not being abreast of the latest trend-movements adds to the anxiety resulting from peer pressure. What are your fears of peer pressure? Take a moment to consider and write your response.

____

____

____

____

____

Believe it or not, peer pressure directly and indirectly influences our daily lives. We all influence one another in some shape or form. Why? We listen and learn from each other. It is human nature in us. Let me share this story with you regarding a learning moment in my life as a youth. The teenage years were a time for me to quickly ascend into "adulthood" because at that stage I was right about everything. I knew everything. And I mean everything. At least that's what my mother told me sarcastically and repeatedly. Arrogantly, I would also debate with friends about information only they knew.

Story: *Four years in high school came and went in the blink of an eye. Peer pressure was at every corner and influenced my decision making. As a case in point, peer pressure influenced the way I perceived the value of homework. While many students viewed homework as a reinforcement of the academic lessons taught in class, my outlook was different. I viewed homework to be time-consuming and robbed me of social life. I eventually understood the value, although difficult. It was difficult saying no to friends when the opportunity presented itself to hang out at the local shopping mall.*

My friends and I often spent late afternoons at the local shopping mall during my junior and senior years in high school. I went along to be "down" with the squad. We would walk around and window-shopped. Other times, we hung out and ate the regular cheeseburgers, pizzas, and cheesesteaks. However, some of my peers had the financial means to purchase trendy clothing and shoes. This was not the case for me. I had a very humble upbringing and lived most of my life financially challenged.

Although I wanted to keep up with my peers on the latest fashioned trends, I could not because my family lacked the finances to support it. I was stuck between keeping up with my peers and the reality of my situation. This was a tough time for me because at that age, staying abreast of the latest fashion trends meant everything. Friends would say to me, "Cop those new Michael Jordan shoes." "They are dope!" Although I was being peer pressured into getting trendy clothing and shoes, I quickly learned life went on even if you do not succumb to it. I did not end up with trendy clothing or shoes, but our friendship remained intact. Why? This is because we were friends. The moral of the story is real friends, accept you for who you are, and it is OK to resist succumbing to peer pressure. ***<u>End.</u>***

In truth, keep your head held high and learn how to accept Jesus Christ in your life. *<u>I have told you these things so that you will be filled with my joy. Yes, your joy will overflow</u>* ***(John 15:11 NLT)***. Your life can still be meaningful without surrendering to peer pressure. Learn to accept yourself the way Jesus Christ created you and its inherited blessings. We may use positive peer pressure in our lives as an encouragement to excel in school, work, or at home. As a case in point, witnessing friends in school achieving excellent grades instills in you, encouragement to pursue the same. Surrounding yourself with this positivity may enable you to reach certain heights once thought unattainable. Standing firm with the beliefs instilled in you can provide the motivation to accomplish anything in life.

"I'm not in this world to live up to your expectations and you're not in this world to live up to mine."

— Bruce Lee

Source: https://www.brainyquote.com/quotes/bruce_lee_153187

Parental Pressure. Cherishing the relationship, you have with your parent(s) is a blessing and is of value. However, there is an added pressure of making your parent(s) proud and to not disappoint them. We are or were in our lives wanting to be just like our parent(s). At the other end of the spectrum, we want or wanted to be absolutely nothing like them. If this statement is true, there is no pressure. However, if you want or wanted to become like mom and/or dad, then you understand fully the stress that comes along with meeting and exceeding expectations. Do you or do not want to become like your parent(s)? Take a moment to consider and write why or why not.

____

____

____

____

____

Parents who strive to provide the best for their children mold them into the adults they feel will succeed in the real world. Finding employment, paying bills, abiding by the laws, and providing for your children are all examples of the "real world." As a youth, the pressure can become a struggle to endure and may impact you negatively. Why are parents doing this if it adds stress in your life? Parents truly want the best for you. Parents work hard to provide and dream of you having a successful life. What happens when mom or dad care too much? Parents, be careful in placing high expectations on your children because this may lead to dissatisfaction and low self-esteem. *Parents*: Encourage and be an encouragement. You are the pillar to their success; support them!

Let us reflect on what the Holy Scripture reveals: *As pressure and stress bear down on me, I find joy in your commands* ***(Psalm 119:143 NLT)***. The scripture begins with a profound statement, "*As pressure and stress bear down on me.*" The deeper meaning indicates the everyday stresses we are forced to deal with. Daily, we are focused on navigating through and around the pressures of decision and consequence. For every decision made, there is an inherent consequence. Positive or negative. For example, as you miss a day of school, there is a backlog of class assignments demanding your attention.

The latter part of the scripture states, "*I find joy in your commands.*" We base the implication of this statement on following the LORD's commandments. The commandments are established as a lifeline to restoring and maintaining our relationship with God. Think of the commandments as a fence around your home, and we are a puppy playing inside the confines of the fence. The confines of the fence are designed to keep the puppy from straying outside the safety of the yard. If the puppy finds itself on the opposite side of the fence, it is faced with a plateau of danger and unforeseen consequences. The fence provides safety for the puppy, just as the commandments do for us. It teaches us what acceptable rules to live by in the eyes of the LORD.

PLACE JESUS CHRIST at the center of your days. As you maneuver through the day, keep Jesus Christ close. Remember, he died for your sins and his abundant love for you is ever so present. Peers and parents may place pressure in your life, but it is Jesus Christ who relieves you of the stress. Trust him and do not be afraid because he is your salvation. Jesus Christ has proven he can manage any crisis and provided loving guidance for his children to follow. Seize this moment as a time to self-discover commitment and dedication. Allow his grace to flow down on your inner-being and succumb to his direction. When you are at a standstill because of peer and parental pressure, turn to Jesus Christ for spiritual uplifting.

Prepare Your Heart for the LORD's Prayer!

Let us pray: Heavenly Father, I come to you today with hopes of a new beginning. I have traveled off the path because of peer and parental pressure. I need your help to refocus on the task at hand. The path you placed forth for me. Who else can be so great in times of need? No one else but you, LORD. My heart is filled with joy and love because of the sacrifices you made for me. You are not a selfish God. You are a God of giving. You gave me peace when I needed it the most. You granted me forgiveness when I sinned. There is no other God in this lifetime or the next that I rather have by my side. Thank you, Father, for everything. Thank you for blessing my family, friends, and everyone who calls out to you in worship. I will praise your name all the days of my life and shout your name to the clouds, so everyone may learn of the mighty God you are. In Jesus' name, in Jesus' name, AMEN!

Building a Relationship with God
1. Begin praying at home
2. Find a place of worship (church)
3. Attend church weekly
4. Join a church ministry and participate monthly
5. Ask Jesus Christ his purpose for you
6. Accept Jesus Christ as your LORD and Savior

Now that you have read about ***Peer and Parental Pressure***, continue reading onto Chapter 11 to learn of the challenges faced regarding ***Competition*** and what the Holy Scripture revealed.

Related Scriptures

Brothers and sisters, we urge you to warn those who are lazy. Encourage those who are timid. Take tender care of those who are weak. Be patient with everyone. **(1 Thessalonians 5:14 NLT)**

In everything we do, we show that we are true ministers of God. We patiently endure troubles and hardships and calamities of every kind. **(2 Corinthians 6:4 NLT)**

So, let's not get tired of doing what is good. At just the right time we will reap a harvest of blessing if we don't give up. **(Galatians 6:9 NLT)**

A servant of the Lord must not quarrel but must be kind to everyone, be able to teach, and be patient with difficult people. **(2 Timothy 2:24 NLT)**

Peer and Parental Pressure Help Resources

https://childdevelopmentinfo.com/ages-stages/teenager-adolescent-development-parenting/teens-peer-pressure/

The U.S. Department of Health & Human Services (1-877-696-6775)

https://www.hhs.gov/ash/oah/adolescent-development/healthy-relationships/healthy-friendships/peer-pressure/index.html

Chapter 11

Competition

Finishing is better than starting. Patience is better than pride. **(*Ecclesiastes 7:8 NLT*)**

What does competition mean to you? The first thing that comes to mind for many people is sporting events. Sports are a popular type of competition. While sports (Basketball, Football, Soccer, Tennis, Rugby, Golf, Boxing, Baseball, Mixed Martial Arts, Cricket, Hockey, CrossFit, etc.) are fun, it may harbor emotions of positivity and negativity. How do you truly feel when you or your team loses a game? Take a moment to consider and write your response.

____

____

____

____

____

For the record, we are disappointed, upset, or sad when the outcome of a sporting event does not go in our favor. Although sports are a popular form of competition, there are other instances. As an example, competing against your siblings to win favoritism from mom or dad. If you grew up with siblings, I could only imagine the types of competition you took part in.

Do you remember arguing over which one of you received the biggest piece of dessert cake? We have competition throughout our entire lives, and it is not solely based on structured events either. When you become adults, it does not mean your competitive spirit ends as a youth. As adults, you compete against coworkers for higher salaries, promotions, job openings, etc. As a case in point, partaking in an important project at work may lead to competition. Perhaps we seek approval from our supervisor or boss to validate how great we are at our jobs. Therefore, we might go above and beyond to outshine coworkers in proving our superior skill sets. These skill sets are frequently tied to salary increases and promotions.

"Oftentimes winning can become an addiction, whether good or bad, to the point where you would rather lose it all before you lose at all."

— Criss Jami

Source: https://www.goodreads.com/quotes/tag/lose-everything

Do you remember your very first form of competition? How did you feel afterward? Take a moment to consider and write your response about how you felt.

____

____

____

____

____

When we compete in anything as a person, we invest our time, energy, and emotions. On the positive side, competition exemplifies play, encourages ingenuity, fosters team building and synergy, promotes problem-solving, supports growth, and most of all, fun! However, on the negative side competition may lead to hostility, anger, injury, lack of self-worth, jealousy, envy, and insecurities. We have witnessed anger in sports where athletes display immense frustration. The open display of frustration may stem from a perceived bad call by a referee or failing to convert the winning play. It is human nature to express emotions over results we perceive as favorable or unfavorable. Have you heard the saying: *The success of one person leads to the failure of another*? Today, we reward and praise winning and discard losing. I want to share a moment with you.

Story: *I took part in many sporting events growing up. These events included basketball, football, soccer, cricket, boxing, and wrestling. The neighborhood kids and I would play basketball at the local park on certain days depending on the weather. If it was raining, we* *played basketball indoors. If it was snowing, we played Tackle Football in the snow. It was all about having fun and losing a game of basketball or football did not affect me. It was just fun, and I did not care to lose earlier in life.*

However, as I got older and teenage hormones came raging into full swing, I realized a change in the way I perceived winning and losing. I developed a feeling of pride. I envied the praise received by peers after winning a game. I embodied competition differently from that moment on. The games were no longer fun, but a "must-win" situation because of pride. This attitude eventually strained close friendships as a youth. I learned over the years to accept winning and losing. I practiced congratulating the winner, carried myself gracefully after winning, and learned the most valuable lesson behind competition. Manage failure after losing a game. As the saying goes, "You can't win them all." ***End.***

The moral of the story is for you to embody competition and do not allow it to change who you are. As a youth, we mimic what we see professional athletes do in their respected sport. Hitting the game-winning basket, hitting a grand-slam home run, or scoring the winning touchdown is the pinnacle of what competition is all about. I ask you this: *Would you mimic what Jesus Christ did on this earth?* Being kind to people. Helping others. Sharing with each other. Loving everyone without prejudice. *For the Kingdom of God is not a matter of what we eat or drink, but of living a life of goodness and peace and joy in the Holy Spirit* ***(Romans 14:17 NLT)***. Jesus Christ did not care which walk of life a person came from. Ethnicity, gender, race, age, social class, disability, etc., did not and does not matter to him. If people needed help, he would extend his love. He will not compete for your love. He gave his life for it through sacrifice. Take a moment to reflect on the sacrifices you have made for people in need.

Let us reflect on what the Holy Scripture reveals: *Finishing is better than starting. Patience is better than pride* ***(Ecclesiastes 7:8 NLT)***. Have you heard the saying, "It does not matter where you start, it matters where you finish?" Competition is living proof of this saying. Many times, in sports we witnessed a team starting out on fire. Scoring point after point and failed to win the game. The scripture emphasizes, *"Finishing is better than starting."* In life, some of us are blessed with abundant riches only to end up poor. The LORD is asking for us to live in harmonious love with each other. There is no need to win at all costs if the consequences result in hurting our brothers or sisters.

He is saying we can all finish together. This means once our work is completed here on earth of serving him through kindness to people, helping others, worshiping Jesus Christ, sharing, and loving everyone without prejudice, we can all finish in Heaven together. The scripture also reads, *"Patience is better than pride."* The LORD is asking for us, his children, to relinquish our pride. Instead, practice patience in him through faith. When we feel an outcome is in our best interest, we quickly rush into a decision, but it only ends in disappointment. Practicing patience through faith enables us to receive approval from Jesus Christ. If a favorable outcome is meant to be for you, it will come to pass.

LEARN TO BE RECEPTIVE to the LORD's grace. Open your heart to this opportunity of redemption. Instead of shying away from competition, embrace it. Allow this instant to enrich your spiritual growth in the LORD. Fairness and kindness practiced in your daily interactions are at the core of your relationship with him. Implementing these two simple words, fairness and kindness into your daily living is the beginning of a lifelong learning experience. The LORD did not teach us to win at all cost but instead practice grace. Take time to submerge into the LORD's presence and become a beacon of his image. Whenever you feel competition has gotten the best of you, remember to live the way Jesus Christ once did, with kindness and grace.

Prepare Your Heart for the LORD's Prayer!

Let us pray: My LORD and savior. Where would I be today without you in my life? How could I have triumphed through difficult times if it were not for your promise? The promise of everlasting love you have for me. There was a time when I thought winning was everything. The only thing that mattered. Thank you for opening my eyes to see the truth.

Forgive me for all the people I might have harmed emotionally because of my selfless portrayal of pride. Once I lived in the darkness of pride, but now the days are brightened by the truth you shined upon me. I pray that I can share with the world my new outlook on life. I pray for your wisdom, so I can teach others the way you want us to live. Enable me to exemplify your love, and from this day forth, I will worship you with abundant belief and faith. In Jesus' name, in Jesus' name, AMEN!

Building a Relationship with God
1. Begin praying at home
2. Find a place of worship (church)
3. Attend church weekly
4. Join a church ministry and participate monthly
5. Ask Jesus Christ his purpose for you
6. Accept Jesus Christ as your LORD and Savior

Now that you have read about ***Competition***, continue reading onto Chapter 12 to learn of the challenges faced regarding ***Poverty*** and what the Holy Scripture revealed.

Related Scriptures

I have observed something else under the sun. The fastest runner doesn't always win the race, and the strongest warrior doesn't always win the battle. The wise sometimes go hungry, and the skillful are not necessarily wealthy. And those who are educated don't always lead successful lives. It is all decided by chance, by being in the right place at the right time. **(Ecclesiastes 9:11 NLT)**

Don't be concerned for your own good but for the good of others. **(1 Corinthians 10:24 NLT)**

You must be compassionate, just as your Father is compassionate. **(Luke 6:36 NLT)**

The Lord demands accurate scales and balances; he sets the standards for fairness. **(Proverbs 16:11 NLT)**

Competition Help Resources

https://kidshealth.org/en/teens/sports-pressure.html

https://www.verywellfamily.com/competition-among-kids-pros-and-cons-4177958

Chapter 12

Poverty

Blessed are those who are generous, because they feed the poor. ***(Proverbs 22:9 NLT)***

Poverty comes in many different shapes and forms. The harsh realities of poverty affect the poor in many ways. People living in poverty might have very little possession or money. Others may lack an adequate educational system, technology, cultural infrastructure, or opportunities for growth. Regardless of the types of poverty you experience, the realities are no different. It hurts!

The ramifications of poverty affect us both physically (malnourishment, disease, sickness, etc.) and mentally (loss of hope, depression, a loss of purpose, etc.). Many people around the world are experiencing poverty or on the brink. Sometimes the thought of not knowing where your next meal is coming from or access to adequate education can cause us to simply give up. I was affected by poverty and although my story may differ from yours; we share a common understanding of its reality. Inadequate access to food, water, shelter, medicine, education, employment, and opportunity for growth are realities experienced around the world. Allow me the opportunity to share with you my story about poverty.

Story: *As a youth, I lived in a place where poverty was affluent. My home was made of plywood for the walls, galvanized zinc for the roof, and cement concrete for the flooring. The plywood was positioned far apart, which meant you could see through the walls. The plywood was placed apart to save on money and avoid exhausting all our resources. My family would place old newspapers between the gaps in the walls. This was done to gain* *privacy and deter neighbors from seeing inside our home. The roof would leak when it rained, and we placed buckets and pots under each leak to prevent items in the home from getting wet.*

The home lacked inside plumbing and reliable electricity. We would take showers outside in an oversized aluminum basin and strategically chose the best times throughout the day to avoid being seen by neighbors. The electricity was intermittent, and we used kerosene lamps throughout the house for lighting. Whenever we were lucky enough to find the money for food, we prepared meals on a small charcoal pit suitable to fit one pot at a time. We also lived with minimal clothing and worn shoes. I remembered we would cut off the back-ends of our shoes to enable everyone in the family to wear the same shoes regardless of the size of our feet.

My family and I often sat around and wondered where the next meal would come from. The truth about hunger is that you rarely have time to think about what to eat tomorrow because you are trying to find food for today. My grandmother was the breadwinner of the family. She would make school uniforms during the week on her foot-pedal sewing machine. Oh, the sound of that machine clunking and clunking was annoying and welcoming at the same time. Why? Because I knew if grandma made school uniforms, she would go to the local market on Saturdays to sell them.

Based on monies earned, she would use it to purchase food and supplies for the upcoming week. The irony was, regardless if she sold any or not, the locals at the market would trade products at the end of the day. To illustrate, school uniforms for a bag of charcoal or a bag of rice. This meant charcoal for cooking meals for the week and rice to fill our bellies. Over the years, we made it out of poverty thanks to the grace of God.

Although things could have been worse, we were fortunate compared to other families in the neighborhood. Most families had far less. I wish I had a winning solution or formula to share with you. Everyone's situation is unique but painful. If you are experiencing poverty, turn to the LORD and ask Him to show you a way out. The road ahead is rocky, but you must not give up because of it. Keep an uplifted spirit throughout this journey because it will serve as a foundation of hope to strengthen you. ***End.***

Jesus Christ saved me. *You satisfy me more than the richest feast. I will praise you with songs of joy* ***(Psalms 63:5 NLT)***. My relationship with Jesus Christ started at a young age. I did not go to church regularly. Our relationship started with me asking why our family was poor and hungry. Who else could I have blamed at that moment? I was only a child. The miracle happened on the day I prayed to Jesus Christ and made a covenant with him. Yes, I made a covenant with Jesus Christ. I said, "Jesus if you get us out of poverty, I will forever accept you in my life and never blame you for anything." Although it took many years and hard work, the miracle happened when poverty took a back seat in my life and Jesus Christ led from the front. Making it out of poverty does not mean you will be wealthy and plenty of money to spend or have access to a great educational system. It means you have just enough to make it through the day. It means you have Jesus Christ this day, the next, and the following.

"You might be poor, your shoes might be broken, but your mind is a palace."

— Frank McCourt

Source: https://www.goodreads.com/quotes/612186-you-might-be-poor-your-shoes-might-be-broken-but

---

There is not a concrete earthly solution to solving poverty. However, steps can be taken to lessen the burden placed on the innocent. Solving poverty demands a worldwide effort. This effort may include identifying the issue, providing cost-effective or free education; share resources as opposed to wasting, creating more jobs, etc. There are countless stories like the one I shared with you. For the millions of people experiencing poverty, each has a story to tell. Is anyone listening to their stories or heard their cries of help? If you were fortunate to make it out of poverty, it does not mean you forget about the ones remaining. Support your local anti-poverty organizations, food banks, churches, family assistance programs, etc. Showing that you care, may influence others to do the same. If you were able to solve poverty, what would you do? Take a moment to consider and write your solution(s).

____

____

____

____

____

Let us reflect on what the Holy Scripture reveals: *Blessed are those who are generous, because they feed the poor* ***(Proverbs 22:9 NLT)***. The scripture asks of us to be generous to the poor. The LORD loves when we care about each other and provide a helping hand. *Blessed are those who are generous* means the LORD favors us when we practice giving. As an example, some people may not feel the need to help a person who does not appear incapable of finding a job on their own. Have you heard this before? "I am not helping them." "They are too lazy to find a job." "They just want free money." The LORD wants us to give without prejudice. We should ask ourselves an honest question: How do we truly know who needs our help without basing it on their appearance? What if you made the wrong assumption when you could have helped?

We have an obligation to ourselves to ensure we do not get taken advantage of by people preying on the generous. The LORD wants you to ask him through prayer for an understanding of situations where you might feel deceived. The latter part of the scripture reads, "*Because they feed the poor.*" The LORD did not say, "*Blessed are those who think about being generous.*" He wants you to follow through on your thoughts of generosity. And you will be blessed because of your actions. We live in a world where we witness generosity as a seasonal event. During the holiday seasons, we give more. Do not base your decision on a special time of year. Pray about it and give it based on what you feel in your heart.

APPROACH JESUS CHRIST and present to him your worries of the world. Do you know what poor people and rich people have in common? God made them both. He knows the rich are living a life of plenty. He also knows the daily anguish of poverty placed upon the poor. God is your nourishment of understanding. He knows your days are filled with uncertainty and self-doubt. Turn to him and ask for a sign of his favor. The strength needed to penetrate through the daily ramifications of poverty is at God's fingertips. A simple gesture of prayer, asking for his favor is a gateway to relinquishing the suffering of poverty.

Prepare Your Heart for the LORD's Prayer!

Let us pray: My LORD and Savior, I pray for everyone who is experiencing poverty. I ask for your control of the challenges placed upon them. I pray that you relieve the poor from poverty. Where there is hunger, please bless them with abundant food. Where there is lost hope, please assure them of your love and promise for them. Lead them to the fountain of prosperity through your miraculous work LORD. Show us how great of a God you truly are. There is no challenge too great for you LORD. I may be poor, but my love for you overflows in riches. Do not give me too much wealth LORD. Do not give me too little wealth LORD. Give me just enough to live an honest and Godly life. When I overcome poverty, please help me to always remember those left behind. Provide me with courage and strength to help as many people as possible. Blessed are those who followed your calling of giving. In Jesus' name, in Jesus' name, AMEN!

Building a Relationship with God

1. Begin praying at home
2. Find a place of worship (church)
3. Attend church weekly
4. Join a church ministry and participate monthly
5. Ask Jesus Christ his purpose for you
6. Accept Jesus Christ as your LORD and Savior

Now that you have read about ***Poverty***, let us move onto the fourth section and begin reading Chapter 13 to learn of the challenges faced regarding ***Cyber Addiction*** and what the Holy Scripture revealed.

Related Scriptures

The Lord makes some poor and others rich; he brings some down and lifts others up. **(1 Samuel 2:7 NLT)**
He lifts the poor from the dust and the needy from the garbage dump. **(Psalms 113:7 NLT)**
The rich and poor have this in common: The Lord made them both. **(Proverbs 22:2 NLT)**
Those who oppress the poor insult their Maker, but helping the poor honors him. **(Proverbs 14:31 NLT)**

Poverty Help Resources

Homeless (1-800-231-6946)
American Family Housing (1-888-600-4357)
The Salvation Army (1-800-728-7825)

SECTION IV

OVERINDULGENCE OF SELF PLEASURES

Those who love pleasure become poor; those who love wine and luxury will never be rich. **(Proverbs 21:17 NLT)**

Chapter 13

Cyber Addiction

At least I can take comfort in this: Despite the pain, I have not denied the words of the Holy One. **(Job 6:10 NLT)**

Nod your head. Yes! Nod your head if you spend more than half your days in front of a technology screen. Whether it is on a laptop, gaming console, smartphone, tablet, virtual reality helmet, video glasses, smartwatches, etc., plenty of time is spent using these gadgets. Although entertaining, you fall into the trap of not being able to separate the virtual world from the one you live in. I am not saying there are no benefits to the virtual world because they are countless. When most of your time is spent in front of a screen, you risk missing out on what is important ... life. Your life is precious, and you should not miss out on its wonderful benefits. *Yes, you should rejoice, and I will share your joy* ***(Philippians 2:18 NLT)***.

Our opportunities to interact with people around us are jeopardized because of it. As a youth, your interpersonal skills are affected and hinder your ability to develop or maintain strong lasting relationships with family, friends, or peers. Spending an extended amount of time in the virtual world may increase exposure to cyberbullying or inappropriate images and content. What is the most practical solution? The solution is not to eliminate exposure to the virtual world. Not at all. The practical solution is to reduce your time spent interacting in it. Make time for your family and friends to interact in person. This form of face-to-face communication helps to build and nurture relationships, increase self-esteem, trust, etc.

The internet offers countless technological benefits to us. In most schools, children use the internet as a learning supplement to their classroom resources. The internet has broken down communication barriers around the world and created an infinite platform for students and teachers in and outside the classroom. The opportunity to use the internet as a tool of learning helps to broaden our scope of knowledge, technical savvy, and the opportunity to be up to date on modern technology. However, when we spend long periods interacting through the virtual world, the inherited side effects may result in cyber addiction. Cyber addiction could potentially damage your health like that of alcohol or drugs. As a case in point, alcohol or drugs and cyber addiction both affect your quality of life.

How can cyber addiction be just as damaging as alcohol or drugs? Take a moment to consider and write your response.

____

____

____

____

"Use the internet wisely for not just the petty enjoyment of your senses, but for the development of your mind as well."

— Abhijit Naskar

Source: https://www.goodreads.com/quotes/tag/internet-addiction

---

Cyber addiction not only consumes most of your time, it places you in isolation and away from what matters in your personal life. For example, this addiction could lead to online compulsive shopping, gambling, or excessive gaming. Some emotional symptoms of cyber addiction may include anxiety, depression, loneliness, mood swings, isolation, or a lost sense of time. Besides emotional symptoms, you may also suffer from physical symptoms including headaches, insomnia, neck pain, or back pain. As my grandparents often said, "Everything is good for you, but only in moderation." I believe if you manage your time spent interacting in the virtual world and the real one, it will benefit you in the long term.

There is a noticeable lifestyle difference between the previous and today's generation of children and physical activities. If you were a child growing up during the previous generation, childhood games were a common involvement. This meant playing outdoors with friends or indoors with board games. Do you remember playing hide and go seek? This was a staple for the previous generation of children. In today's generation, children are more determined to play video games indoors. A benefit of being a part of today's generation is growing up to become more tech-savvy compared to previous generations. This is because of easy access to technologies, i.e. laptop, gaming console, smartphone, tablet, virtual reality helmet, video glasses, smartwatches, etc. Information is readily available at your fingertips. However, due to the inherent benefits of these technologies and the required interaction time, you are presented with the risk of cyber addiction.

The days of children playing outdoors are becoming a distant memory because of easy access to cyber technologies. Spending most of your days indoors interacting with cyber technologies result in less physical activities. The lack of physical activities lends itself to obesity in children, health problems, and withdrawal. As a case in point, children who are shy communicating with peers may find they hide behind cyber technologies and are unable to fully develop his or her personal communication skills. A balance of outdoor activities and cyber technology interaction are positive steps in the right direction towards fighting cyber addiction.

Let us reflect on what the Holy Scripture reveals: *At least I can take comfort in this: Despite the pain, I have not denied the words of the Holy One* ***(Job 6:10 NLT)***. The scripture starts by emphasizing the word *"comfort."*

What does it mean by, *"At least I can take comfort?"* The scripture is revealing that regardless of the struggles you are experiencing, you can find comfort in the LORD. Comfort may take the shape of praying to the LORD, reading the Bible's Holy Scriptures, or sharing your daily life-struggles with a prayer or worship group in a church ministry.

The second part of the scripture mentioned *"pain."* The scripture is acknowledging the presence of pain in our lives. The latter part of the scripture touched on, *"Not denying the words of the LORD."* It is saying regardless of the looming life challenges, i.e. cyber addiction; do not lose sight of the meaning behind the LORD's words. For example, if you are faced with insurmountable challenges, do not forget the LORD is there with you. He will not give you more than you can handle. Therefore, remain close to the LORD by accepting his Holy Words of promise. Jesus Christ was sacrificed for our sins because he loves his children, you.

THE LORD IS YOUR KNIGHT IN ARMOR equipped to protect his people of faith. When you are fatigued and drained from the deceptions of this world, take a moment to reflect on what is important in your life. The biggest danger of deception is falling victim. Deception is another form of telling lies, except victims are intentionally misled to believe a lie is a truth. The deception of cyber addiction is unpleasantly real. Ask the LORD for discernment to interpret the lies of cyber addiction. Where you have lost the distinction between reality and the virtual world, let the LORD show you signs of direction. Transition your life to worshiping and praising the LORD. When you practice this act, you will not have time to feel sorry for yourself because your thoughts are occupied with worshiping and praising of him.

Prepare Your Heart for the LORD's Prayer!

Let us pray: LORD, grant me the courage to break away these chains of cyber addiction. Allow me the opportunity to gracefully transition into a new chapter of my life. A chapter where there is a balance between cyber technology-interaction and the reality of friends and family. I pray that I continue to nurture these relationships, LORD. How else can I triumph if not for you leading the way? I ask for your guidance in all that I do and forgiveness where I fall short of your expectations. Please help the children who are going through this addiction. Help them to find a path to recovery. For those who are lost, please discover them LORD and bring them to the forefront of salvation. Once I was lost, but you heard my prayer of help. Thank you, LORD, for the pillow of hope and granting favors to my prayers. I have found my way to you. I pray my days are filled with everlasting blessings. In Jesus' name, in Jesus' name, AMEN!

Building a Relationship with God

1. Begin praying at home
2. Find a place of worship (church)
3. Attend church weekly
4. Join a church ministry and participate monthly
5. Ask Jesus Christ his purpose for you
6. Accept Jesus Christ as your LORD and Savior

Now that you have read about ***Cyber Addiction***, continue reading onto Chapter 14 to learn of the challenges faced regarding ***Alcohol and Drug Abuse*** and what the Holy Scripture revealed.

Related Scriptures

Commit everything you do to the Lord. Trust him, and he will help you. **(Psalms 37:5 NLT)**

Please, Lord, rescue me! Come quickly, Lord, and help me. **(Psalms 40:13 NLT)**

God is our refuge and strength, always ready to help in times of trouble. **(Psalms 46:1 NLT)**

Two people are better off than one, for they can help each other succeed. **(Ecclesiastes 4:9 NLT)**

Cyber Addiction Help Resources

https://www.psycom.net/iadcriteria.html

https://www.helpguide.org/articles/addictions/smartphone-addiction.htm/

https://talbottcampus.com/teens-and-internet-addiction/

Chapter 14

Alcohol and Drug Abuse

The temptations in your life are no different from what others experience. And God is faithful. He will not allow the temptation to be more than you can stand. When you are tempted, he will show you a way out so that you can endure. **(1 Corinthians 10:13 NLT)**

Why do people consume alcohol or drugs? Although there are many answers to this question, the consensus is alcohol and drugs make us feel great, fantastic! Do you remember the first time testing your boundaries with alcohol or drugs? Perhaps you knew of someone who indulged and now they are struggling with addiction. Maybe you have never leaped into temptation. Regardless if you never partook, neither are a good habit to pick up. The habits of consuming alcohol and drugs have ruined many marriages, relationships, families, careers, health, finances, life dreams, etc. Let us use finances to illustrate the case in point. A person who regularly consumes alcohol or drugs may find themselves spending more and more money over time due to increased intake and addiction. This person may not have realized the monies being wasted until it is too late. In many common cases, the person ends up missing monthly bill payments and results in a snowball effect of financial problems.

One thing is for certain. No one ever thought the first time indulging in alcohol or drugs came with consequences. Most people practice this habit because it relieves them from stress or anxiety. Some people consume alcohol and drugs because it enables them to forget about their problems. Temporarily at least. The more you depend on these substances to relieve you of the problems of the world; you are in jeopardy of developing substance abuse and begin down a dark path to addiction.

"An over-indulgence of anything, even something as pure as water, can intoxicate."

— Criss Jami

Source: https://www.goodreads.com/quotes/464065-an-over-indulgence-of-anything-even-something-as-pure-as-water

---

Consuming alcohol or drugs places us at risk for many problems. Encountering legal troubles and poor academic grades in school are two of the many consequences. Parents want what is best for their children and standing by idle is not an option. Parents have an obligation to teach children about making the right choices and the dangers of long-term health issues (physical and emotional) later in life. The first step is to keep an open dialogue. This is key to breaching the communication barrier. The generational gaps are evident between parents and children. Some parents experience much difficulty when attempting to find a breakthrough. What can you do as a parent to combat this challenge? Do not stop trying. This is the most critical action and never succumb to failure. Reaching a breakthrough may result in saving your child's life and preserving their future. Allow me to share a story with you.

Story: *There was a time in my life when I thought the taste of alcohol was just terrible! Trying different alcoholic beverages did not convince me either. I tried cheap and expensive brands, but my taste buds did not fall for it. I found myself drinking more of it, although the taste was unpleasant. Why would I keep consuming a beverage I could not tolerate? The answer was peer pressure. I was too weak and gave into peer pressure. I consumed alcohol whenever friends and I went out for a night into town. Eventually, the taste was not so bad. It became fun and a must-do whenever friends and I went out to local bars and nightclubs. The nights were not fun without the consumption of alcohol. The more alcohol consumed meant fun and laughter for everyone. This was the beginning of alcohol abuse.*

I welcomed the feeling of relaxation and enjoyment. The more I consumed alcohol, the more I enjoyed the short-term benefits. The long-term effects, however, were not welcomed. Waking up late for work, morning sickness (hangover), weight gain, and prolonged tiredness were only some of the consequences. I learned quickly and early in life that consuming alcohol came with short-term benefits and long-term consequences. I was very fortunate to avoid more serious life-changing consequences such as health problems or legal troubles. The path-to-solution I took was to drink in moderation and avoided relying on alcohol for happiness. I remained positive and lived one day at a time while progressively reducing my alcohol intake. ***End***.

Do you know of someone who has a high tolerance for alcohol and/or drugs? Perhaps this person is you. If you answered yes, take a moment to reflect and write how it affected your life.

____

____

____

____

____

A person who starts out consuming alcohol and drugs for the alleviation of problems develops a high tolerance.

When this happens, you need to consume more to achieve the same desired effects. We call this substance abuse. Once your body becomes dependent on these substances, it is hard to recover without professional intervention. Admitting you have a substance abuse problem is the first step to recovery. *Gone are the joys of wine and song; alcoholic drink turns bitter in the mouth* ***(Isaiah 24:9 NLT)***. A person with substance abuse problems may not realize the dangers placed on the innocent. Danger includes operating an automobile while intoxicated. This unfortunate practice has taken and ruined many lives. Do not make this mistake. If you are on this path, it is not too late to stop. Seek professional help before you hurt others or yourself. You do not have to take this journey to recovery on your own.

Let us reflect on what the Holy Scripture reveals: *The temptations in your life are no different from what others experience. And God is faithful. He will not allow the temptation to be more than you can stand. When you are tempted, he will show you a way out so that you can endure* **(1 Corinthians 10:13 NLT)**. The scripture began by stating a comparison between different lives. The scripture states, "*Temptations in your life are no different* *from what others experience."* Focus on the word *"temptation."* The LORD is telling us that everyone, including you, faces the same temptations other people face. It does not matter if you are rich, poor, male, female, old, or young. Temptation has no preference. Temptation does not care which walk of life you came from.

We are all fair game. For instance, the temptation of alcohol and drugs is an invitation to everyone. If you abuse these substances, there are consequences. The LORD wants to get this point across to you. The LORD also wants to remind us he is faithful. Yes. The LORD is faithful to us. This means he will not ignore our cries for help. The second sentence in the scripture reads, *"He (the LORD) will not allow the temptation to be more than you can stand."* We are all faced with temptation daily. The LORD has proven that whenever we are at our weakest, our last gasp for hope, he will jump right in and ease us of the burden. The LORD tests our faith through trials.

When we are bombarded with unfortunate situations and challenges, this is the time to dig deep into our bag of faith and pray to God for strength to endure. This is a great opportunity to build your relationship with God. Remember, these temptations are only steps in a relationship-building exercise. The more faith and trust you place in the LORD, the more you triumph. The last part of the scripture reads, *"When you are tempted, he will show you a way out so that you can endure."* This means when you succumb to temptation, the LORD is there to rescue you and place a path in front of you to follow. Keep praying to him and ask for help. He will not disappoint you.

BE ON GUARD against distractions of self-pleasure. The pleasures of self-medication are abundant in this world. Too often the simplistic values of right and wrong are blurred between our longings for immediate relief and permanent solution to our daily life-struggles. The easy, temporary solution is to rely on alcohol and drugs for instant gratification. But the LORD wants you to stop this practice. He wants you to rely on him for a more permanent solution to the problems in your life. There are no negative side effects of worshiping the LORD. The long-term benefits of turning to the LORD consist of peace, joy, and everlasting life. His abundant love extends beyond this world. The life negated of alcohol and drug abuse is within sight. Let him show you the way through your faith in him.

Prepare Your Heart for the LORD's Prayer!

Let us pray: My LORD, show me a way through this struggle of alcohol and drugs. I have learned that overcoming this struggle requires tough decision-making on my part. The toughest decision is to admit I am not strong enough to succeed on my own. I need a God of patience. I am stubborn LORD. The indulgence of alcohol and drugs provides me with a false benefit of relief to all daily life-struggles and I am addicted. My friends and family are paying the price of disappointment and shame. Lift me from the debts of this struggle LORD. Help me reclaim a life of happiness and love which once belonged to me. I am ready to take a leap of faith into your arms LORD. In Jesus' name, in Jesus' name, AMEN!

Building a Relationship with God

1. Begin praying at home
2. Find a place of worship (church)
3. Attend church weekly
4. Join a church ministry and participate monthly
5. Ask Jesus Christ his purpose for you
6. Accept Jesus Christ as your LORD and Savior

Now that you have read about ***Alcohol and Drug Abuse***, continue reading onto Chapter 15 to learn of the challenges faced regarding ***Premarital Sex*** and what the Holy Scripture revealed.

Related Scriptures
You say, "I am allowed to do anything" - but not everything is good for you. And even though "I am allowed to do anything," I must not become a slave to anything. **(1 Corinthians 6:12 NLT)** But you must be careful so that your freedom does not cause others with a weaker conscience to stumble. **(1 Corinthians 8:9 NLT)** Instead, clothe yourself with the presence of the Lord Jesus Christ. And don't let yourself think about ways to indulge your evil desires. **(Romans 13:14 NLT)** Wine produces mockers; alcohol leads to brawls. Those led astray by drink cannot be wise. **(Proverbs 20:1 NLT)**

Alcohol and Drug Abuse Help Resources
Marijuana Anonymous (1-800-766-6779) Alcohol Treatment Referral Hotline (24 hours) (1-800-252-6465) Cocaine Hotline (24 hours) (1-800-262-2463) Drug Abuse National Helpline (1-800-662-4357) National Association for Children of Alcoholics (1-888-554-2627) Ecstasy Addiction (1-800-468-6933)

Chapter 15

Premarital Sex

When doubts filled my mind, your comfort gave me renewed hope and cheer. ***(Psalm 94:19 NLT)***

Temptation is all around us. Temptation has no prejudice and presents itself to us all. Regardless if you are an adult or youth, the allure of temptation is all too real. The internet, television, or local schools exposes our youth to influences pertaining to premarital sex. Why do we consider or give in to this temptation? Is it because other people around us are actively partaking? Some might say, "My friends are doing it, why can't I?" Perhaps you are just curious. There is nothing wrong with being curious, however, it is what we do with this curiosity that gets us in trouble. To illustrate, watching a sexually explicit video while you are a youth may spark interest and lead you down a path of self-discovery.

Reenacting what you viewed on the internet or television is not a wise decision. The opportunity is here for you to get back on the chosen path. *Oh, what joy for those whose disobedience is forgiven, whose sin is put out of sight* ***(Psalms 32:1 NLT)***. There are consequences you may not have considered such as sexually transmitted diseases or unplanned pregnancies. If you are a minor considering this act, consult an adult, seek professional counseling, and/or speak to a local church ministry to learn more and why you should wait until you are of legal age and married.

"If a man says he is Christian, yet he has no problems knocking you up, having premarital sex or living in sin with you, then you have to ask yourself, "What version of Christ does he believe in?"

— Shannon L. Alder

Source: https://www.goodreads.com/quotes/778445-if-a-man-says-he-is-christian-yet-he-has

---

This is an important decision in your life. Feeling you are an adult and being an adult are two different things. Do not partake in adult activities if you are not old enough to deal with the consequences. Praying to God and seeking professional counseling is a precautionary measure if you are contemplating the act of premarital sex. Parents, communicate with your children regarding this issue and explain the consequences of premarital sex. Talk about the importance of your child's future and the value of receiving an education. You may also monitor your children's activities to discourage premarital sex.

The youths are inquisitive and learn from observation. Occasionally, your passion and excitement for each other get the better of you. Some may say, "I will be careful." "I will not get pregnant or contract a disease." The truth is abstinence is the best safety precaution in dealing with any doubts or apprehensions. My grandmother always said, "Play with fire and one day you will get burned." If you contracted a disease through premarital sex, you need to seek medical attention and counseling. This is a manageable situation and deserves your attention-to-detail in finding medical treatment and solutions.

What if you truly feel you are old enough to understand and accept the inherited consequences? What if you got pregnant or contracted a disease as a result? If you are a youth dealing with any consequences of premarital sex, please remain positive. Seek professional and medical consultation. There are also available sex educational programs covering sexual abstinence, reproductive health, birth control, etc. You can still achieve anything you want in life. Although this requires more dedication, your personal and family goals remain attainable.

The responsibilities of a young parent do not and should not deter you from pursuing your lifelong dreams. While challenging, many young parents have gone on to achieve personal and professional goals in life. Having a support staff of family and friends helps significantly. If you are a young parent, do not be discouraged. Hold your head high and reach out to professional services and churches in your local community supporting underage parenting. What are your thoughts on premarital sex? Should you wait? Take a moment to consider and write your response.

____

____

____

____

____

Let us reflect on what the Holy Scripture reveals: *When doubts filled my mind, your comfort gave me renewed hope and cheer* ***(Psalm 94:19 NLT).*** The scripture sheds light on the word, "*doubt.*" It reads, *"When doubts filled my mind."* The LORD knows we all have doubts. As humans, we have doubts when the truth or reality of a situation is called into question. Doubt raises uncertainty and robs us of our confidence, hope, or joy. As an example, we may doubt overcoming life obstacles and succumb to the uncertainty by giving up.

The LORD does not want you to give up because you are facing a tough situation. He wants you to cast away all doubts and come to him for guidance. You might have many doubts floating around in your head, but there is a solution. Ask Jesus Christ through prayer for your solution. The second part of the verse reads, *"Your comfort gave me renewed hope and cheer."* Approaching the LORD through prayer comforts us. It assures us our Father is listening to our concerns. For instance, think of people venting to each other about a problem. Sometimes they do not want your opinion; they just want you to listen. However, the LORD not only listens to your problems, but he also intervenes and helps you to overcome them. What an amazing God we have!

BE THANKFUL for the days of wisdom, direction, and self-reflection. The LORD wants you to transition your mind away from the temptations of premarital sex and focus on him. Whenever your thoughts wander off contemplating premarital sex, remember you have a loving father that knows your heart. He has placed a pure heart in you and understands the temptations of premarital sex. While you are busy maneuvering your thoughts on a decision, the LORD has found a solution for you. Remain in deep prayer with him and resist the urge of succumbing to your desires. The weather might change. Fashion trends might change. But the LORD's love for you will remain unchanged throughout eternity.

Prepare Your Heart for the LORD's Prayer!

Let us pray: Thank you LORD for this opportunity to be here in your loving presence. The opportunity to share with you the struggle I am facing at this very moment. Help me to surpass this struggle and to share with others the love-of-caring you gave me. I know the temptation will always be around the corner yearning for my indecisions. Please provide me the willpower to say, "No". I understand a great responsibility has been bestowed upon me. I need you, LORD. Show me what an amazing God you are. Help me find balance of life's responsibilities and never forget you are always beside me, behind me, and in front of me. I do not want another day without you in my life LORD. Thank you for bestowing comfort upon me. In Jesus' name, in Jesus' name, AMEN!

Building a Relationship with God

1. Begin praying at home
2. Find a place of worship (church)
3. Attend church weekly
4. Join a church ministry and participate monthly
5. Ask Jesus Christ his purpose for you
6. Accept Jesus Christ as your LORD and Savior

Now that you have read about ***Premarital Sex***, let us **conclude** with what we discovered regarding our daily life-struggles and what the Holy Scriptures revealed.

Related Scriptures

By standing firm, you will win your souls. **(Luke 21:19 NLT)**

Don't let evil conquer you but conquer evil by doing good. **(Romans 12:21 NLT)**

Dear friend, don't let this bad example influence you. Follow only what is good. Remember that those who do good prove that they are God's children, and those who do evil prove that they do not know God. **(3 John 1:11 NLT)**

Trust in the Lord with all your heart; do not depend on your own understanding. **(Proverbs 3:5 NLT)**

Premarital Sex Help Resources

Seek advice from your local church ministry and/or pastor

Conclusion

Listen to his instructions and store them in your heart
***(Job 22:22 NLT)*.**

Most adults probably remember the daily life-struggles encountered as a youth. Yet they place emphasis on the youth of today to somehow maneuver through it all effortlessly. We must share our personal experiences with a deeper duty of care. Just as Jesus Christ did for us, we should be a pillar of trust for our youth. I want to take a moment and share with you a short story about a young restaurant waiter and his triumph through faith in God.

<u>Story</u>: *On a Friday night after a difficult week of work, I made my way to a local restaurant for a bite to eat. Although it was less than an hour, the wait-time for a seat seemed like an eternity. The pleasant aroma of foods stimulating the restaurant made the wait worthwhile. The hostess voiced my name over the intercom system and expeditiously escorted me to a table. The restaurant erupted with conversations and laughter. The room echoed of excitement and customers enjoyed the triumph of making it through the workweek.*

I imagined the loud conversations to be an acceptance of tasty pleasures and the wonderful selection of foods as the reward. A male waiter approached and introduced himself a few minutes after being seated. He seemed polite and filled with self-confidence. I ordered a beverage of choice and he suggested an appetizer to kick off my dining experience. He then proceeded to inscribe on a notepad my meal order for the evening.

The waiter appeared to be a few years removed from his youth. I asked his perception of working as a waiter, prompting the conversation. He described working as a waiter to be ideal for his outgoing personality. His outgoing personality allowed him to meet and interact with people from many walks of life. Our conversation evolved on a personal level as the evening progressed. The young waiter was knowledgeable about his career field and enthusiastically shared his experiences.

The first revelation of the night came when he spoke of living in Foster Homes throughout his young life. He was ready to share his story, surprisingly. He spoke cautiously and carefully about living in Foster Homes. Perhaps a bit reserved to avoid reopening of emotional wounds. His struggles of living in Foster Homes did not diminish his motivation and self-confidence based on my observations.

The wisdom and outlook on life led me to express a sense of belief in him. He seemed destined to achieve anything in life. Perhaps he was ordained to become an owner of a restaurant or Chief Executive Officer of a company. He seemed prepared and equipped for success. Our conversation about life progressed, as the minutes past. The apparent struggles of young people surviving in a world diluted with countless obstacles and temptations are unmistakable.

The Holy Spirit moved me to ask a personal question about his relationship with the LORD. The approach to asking this question was not without hesitation because of the atmosphere. Nonetheless, there is never a more convenient place or moment to talk about our Heavenly Father, than the present. "I am impressed with how far you came in life and you have a good head on your shoulders," I began to speak. "How are you on the other side of your life?" I asked. "Do you have a balance?" "Meaning, do you have God in your life?" He replied, "Yes," without hesitation. That was the second revelation of the night. I was relieved, impressed, and happy to learn he had Jesus Christ in his life.

Millions of young adults accepted Jesus Christ in their lives. However, witnessing one of those stories in person was memorable and a blessing. I know this young man will succeed in life. Why? The LORD is at the forefront and leading him along a righteous path. I never told him I was authoring a book intended to reach the youth who had experienced or experiencing daily life-struggles in their lives. I simply did not want our conversation in writing a book to overshadow our conversation of the LORD in his life.

His life story inspired me and confirmed there is a need for this book and its biblical reflection of the daily life-struggles experienced by our youth. His life story portrayed a youth overcoming life obstacles through perseverance and faith in God. The conversation on that busy Friday night was a learning experience and the LORD was responsible for that moment of enlightenment. Thank you, LORD. ***End.***

I truly hope and pray you have gained knowledge and insight into these daily life-struggles. I know in my heart there is a need for people to lend a helping hand to those who are searching for answers in this world. This book covered significant daily life-struggles and each of the struggles was explained thoroughly and supported by biblical scriptures to highlight its relevance and applicability. If you have biblical questions, concerns, or a desire to learn more about the chapters you have read, please feel free to contact your local church ministry and/or pick up a copy of the Holy Bible to learn more about the scriptures.

Just as Jesus Christ followed messages-of-instruction from his Holy Father, the Holy Bible is filled with powerful messages applicable to your daily living.

Remember to follow the six-step process listed throughout this book of building a relationship with God. As you might recall, the six steps included praying at home, finding a place of worship, attending church on a weekly basis, participating in a church ministry, asking Jesus Christ his purpose for you, and accepting him as your LORD and Savior. The daily life-struggles you face are real and facing them alone is extremely challenging. Developing the courage to ask for help is even more difficult. This is normally the case if you are accustomed to problem-solving without intervention from others. The road ahead is full of uncertainties when dealing with daily life-struggles of the world. Asking for and accepting help may lessen the burden.

BE FAITHFUL under all circumstances that life places upon you. Although you may not see proof immediately during times of uncertainty, maintaining strong faith and belief that Jesus Christ is working on a solution for you is paramount. "Seeing is believing," as the old saying goes. But faith is exercising complete confidence and trust in the LORD. A person who lacks faith may question the Holy Bible. This occurs when our perception of reality does not coincide with our beliefs of biblical accounts. People were not born with faith. A life journey of trials and tribulations led them to develop it. Whenever you begin to search in your heart for a sense of belonging, call out to Jesus Christ for his intervention. Allow him to fill your spirit with what you have been lacking. *Now, my son, listen to me. Do exactly as I tell you* ***(Genesis 27:8 NLT)***.

Prepare Your Heart for the LORD's Prayer!

Let us pray: My LORD, my Savior, my Friend, my Champion; thank you for this precious moment to share my thoughts, my heart with you. I feel uplifted when I hear your Holy Name. I pray that each day your blessings rain down upon me. Help me to develop a faith in you that is unbreakable. Give me the strength to make it through this day and the ones to come. I know now you are intertwined in every aspect of my being. Praise God! Thank you for providing me the opportunity to open my heart to you and accepting you as my King of Kings and LORD of LORDs. Enable me to share my knowledge of you with the world. Help me to be courageous and may your Holy Spirit fill impenetrable hearts with your love, and peace. In Jesus' name, in Jesus' name, AMEN!

Help Resources

Alcohol and Drug Abuse Help Resources

Marijuana Anonymous (1-800-766-6779)
Alcohol Treatment Referral Hotline (24 hours) (1-800-252-6465)
Drug Abuse National Helpline (1-800-662-4357)
National Association for Children of Alcoholics (1-888-554-2627)

Bullying Help Resources

https://www.stopbullying.gov/

https://www.stopbullying.gov/get-help-now/index.html

Child Abuse Help Resources

National Sexual Assault Hotline (1-800-656-HOPE (4673)

National Child Abuse Hotline (1-800-4-A-CHILD (422-4453)

Exploitation of Children (1-800-843-5678)

Competition Help Resources

https://kidshealth.org/en/teens/sports-pressure.html

https://www.verywellfamily.com/competition-among-kids-pros-and-cons-4177958

Cyber Addiction Help Resources

https://www.psycom.net/iadcriteria.html

https://www.helpguide.org/articles/addictions/smartphone-addiction.htm/

https://talbottcampus.com/teens-and-internet-addiction

Depression and Suicide Help Resources

Suicide Prevention Hotline (1-800-827-7571)
Suicide Hotline (1-800-SUICIDE) (784-2433)
National Suicide Prevention Lifeline 1-800-273-TALK (8255)
National Depression Association (1-800-826-3632)

Eating Disorders Help Resources

Eating Disorders Awareness and Prevention (1-800-931-2237)

https://www.nationaleatingdisorders.org/help-support/contact-helpline

Emotional Health Help Resources

https://www.samhsa.gov/data/report/2018-national-directory-mental-health-treatment-facilities (1-877-726-4727)

http://www.nacbt.org/contact-us/

https://www.apa.org/helpcenter/ (800) 374-2721)

Crisis Call Center (1-800-273-8255) or text ANSWER to 839863

Peer and Parental Pressure Help Resources

https://childdevelopmentinfo.com/ages-stages/teenager-adolescent-development-parenting/teens-peer-pressure/

The U.S. Department of Health & Human Services (1-877-696-6775)

https://www.hhs.gov/ash/oah/adolescent-development/healthy-relationships/healthy-friendships/peer-pressure/index.html

Poverty Help Resources

The Salvation Army (1-800-728-7825)
https://www.usa.gov/benefits
USA Government Benefits (1-844-872-4681)

Premarital Sex Help Resources

Seek advice from your local church ministry and/or pastor

Self-Esteem and Body Image Help Resources

Eating Disorders Awareness and Prevention (1-800-931-2237)
https://kidshealth.org/en/teens/body-image.html

Self-Identity Help Resources

https://www.goodtherapy.org/learn-about-therapy/issues/identity-issues

1-888-563-2112 ext. 1

https://www.goodtherapy.org/contact-us.html

https://www.mirror-mirror.org/email.htm

https://www.mirror-mirror.org/identity-and-self-esteem.htm

Single-Parent Households Help Resources

http://www.singlemoms.org/housing-resources-for-single-mothers/

https://singlemothersgrants.org/tanf-cash-assistance-for-single-mothers/

The Salvation Army (1-800-728-7825)

https://www.usa.gov/benefits

USA Government Benefits (1-844-872-4681)

Teen Pregnancy Help Resources

American Pregnancy Association (1-800-672-2296)

Planned Parenthood Federation of America (1-800-230-PLAN)

https://americanpregnancy.org/unplanned-pregnancy/pregnant-teen/

https://www.pregnancybirthbaby.org.au/financial-support-for-teenage-parents

Acknowledgements

Thank you, LORD for granting me the opportunity to author this book. Thank you for using me as a tool in reaching others. And, thank you for placing me here on this earth to witness your miracles through healing, love, and grace. I am grateful to you for a supporting and loving family, and may you bless them as you have blessed me.

www.ingramcontent.com/pod-product-compliance
Lightning Source LLC
Chambersburg PA
CBHW022130080426
42734CB00006B/304

* 9 7 8 1 9 7 0 0 5 5 0 3 0 *